STRESS RELIEF

MOTIVATIONAL Coloring For:

____

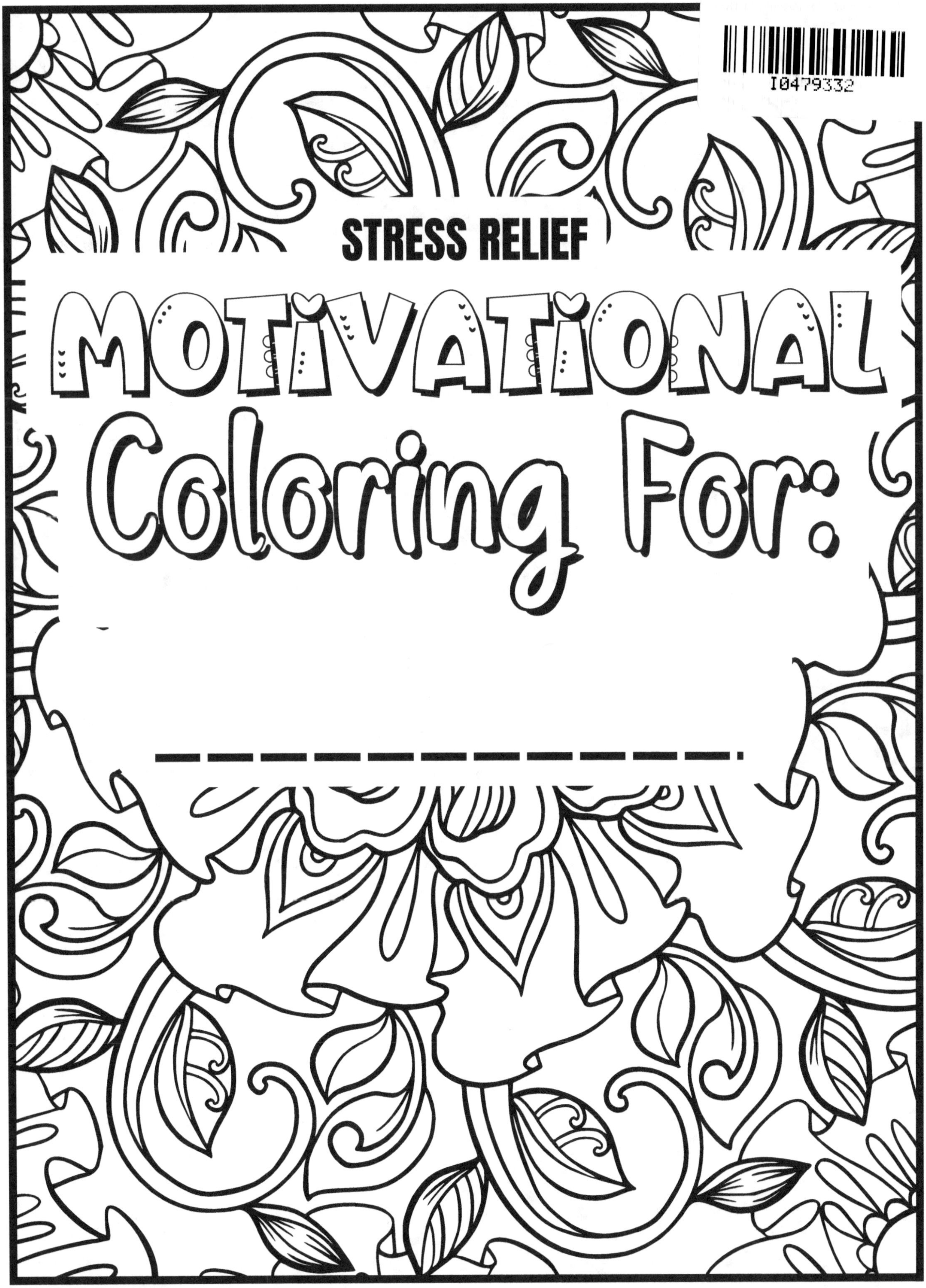

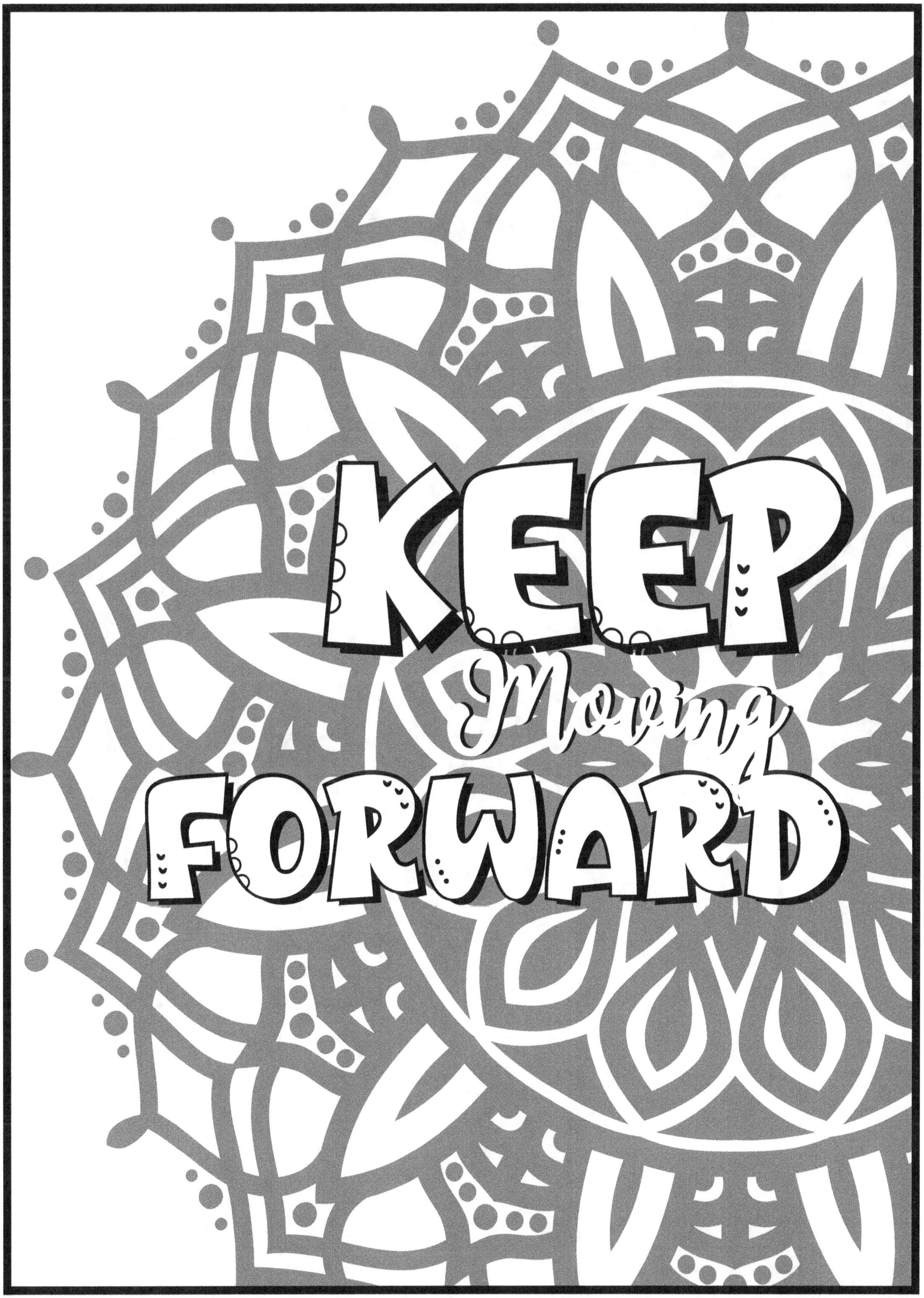
KEEP
Moving
FORWARD

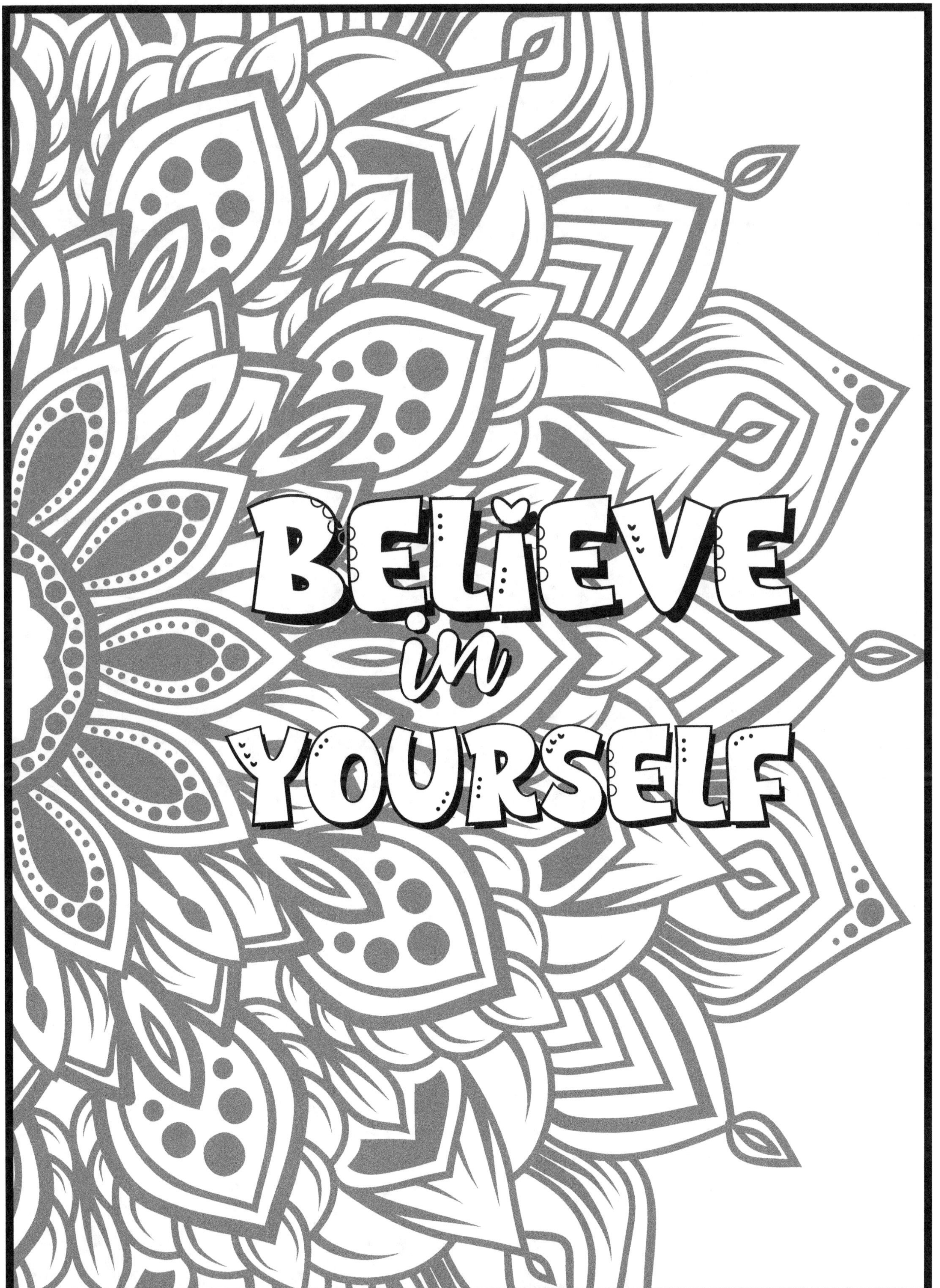
BELIEVE
in
YOURSELF

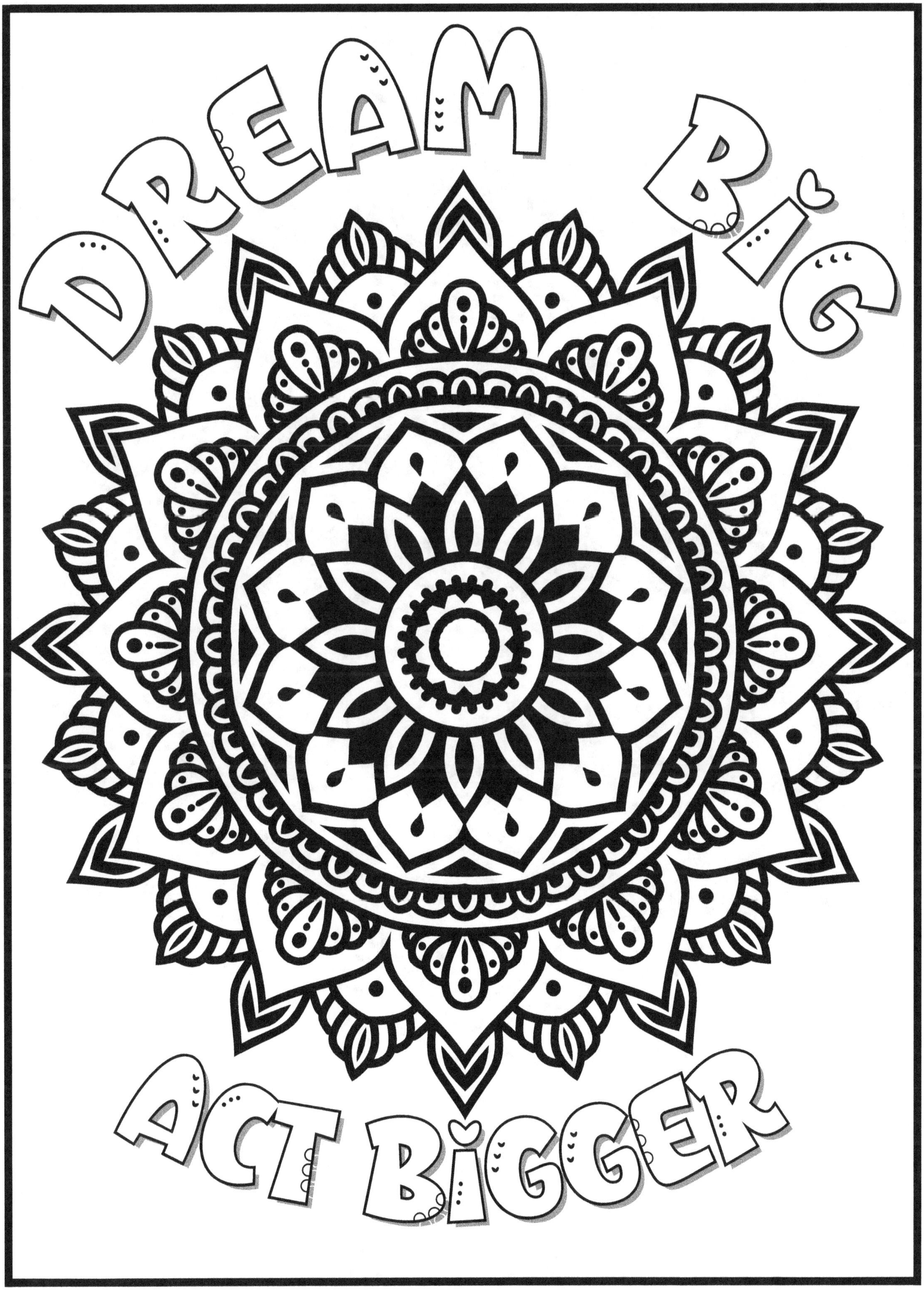
DREAM BIG
ACT BIGGER

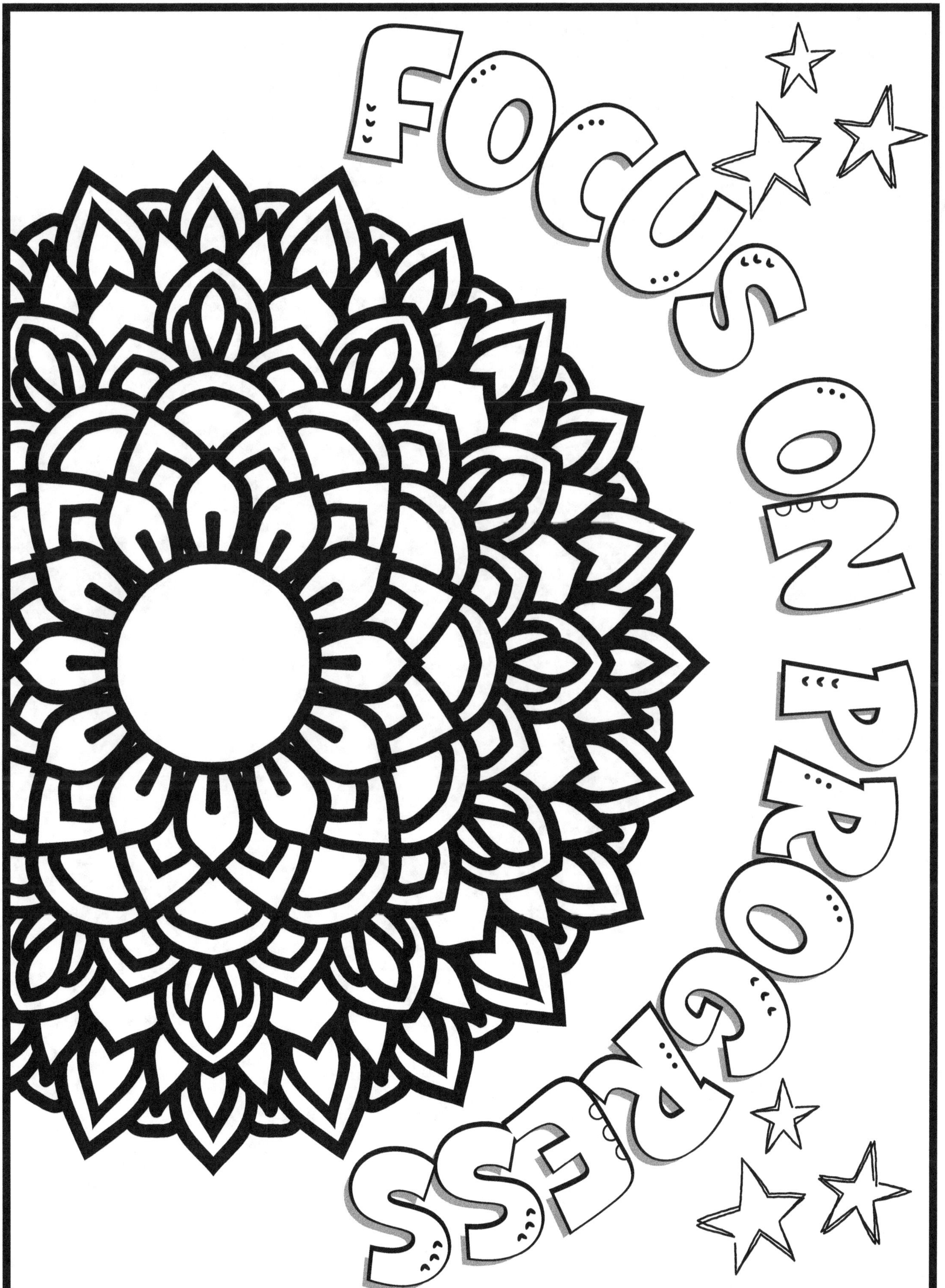
FOCUS ON PROGRESS

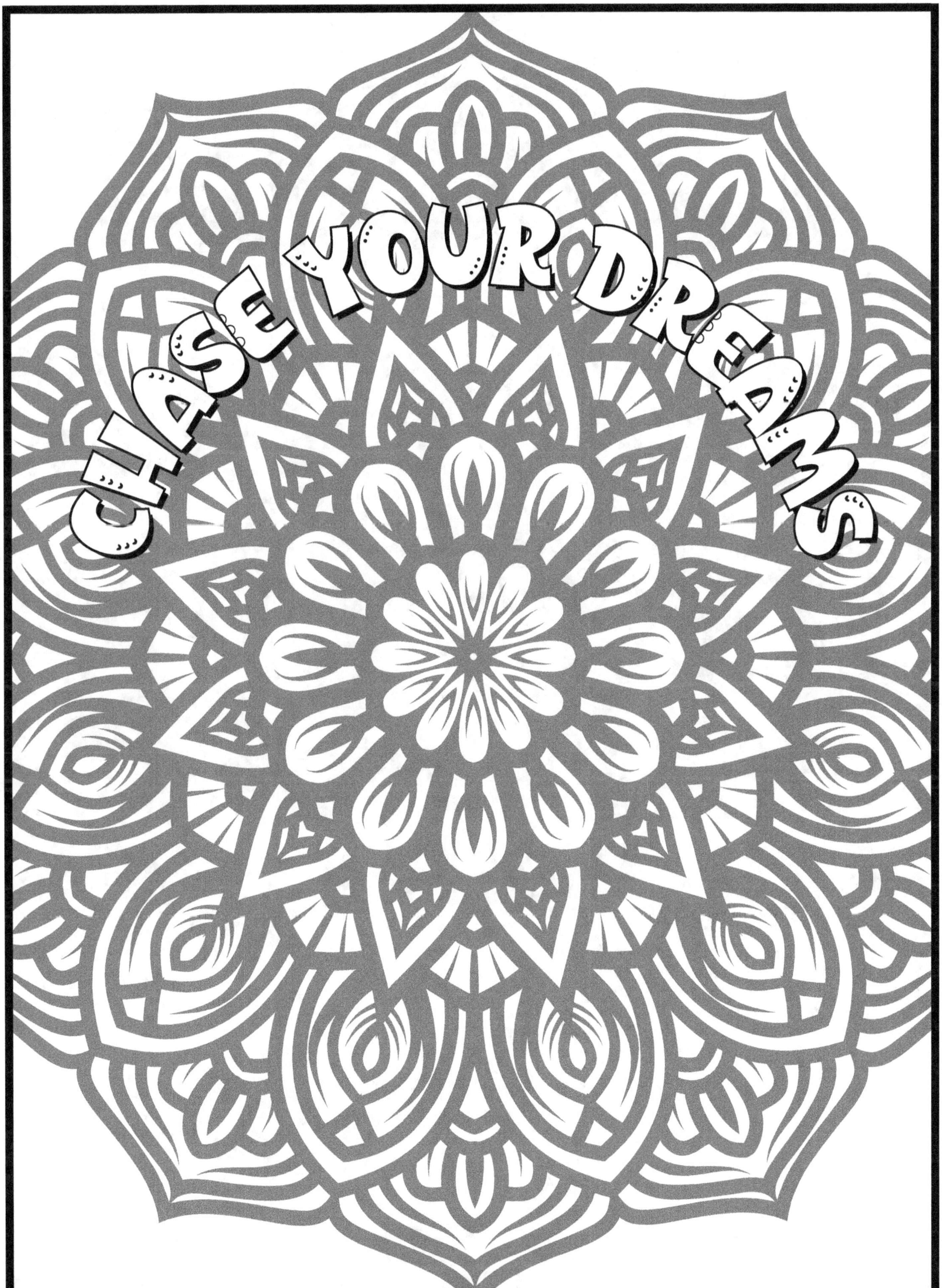
CHASE YOUR DREAMS

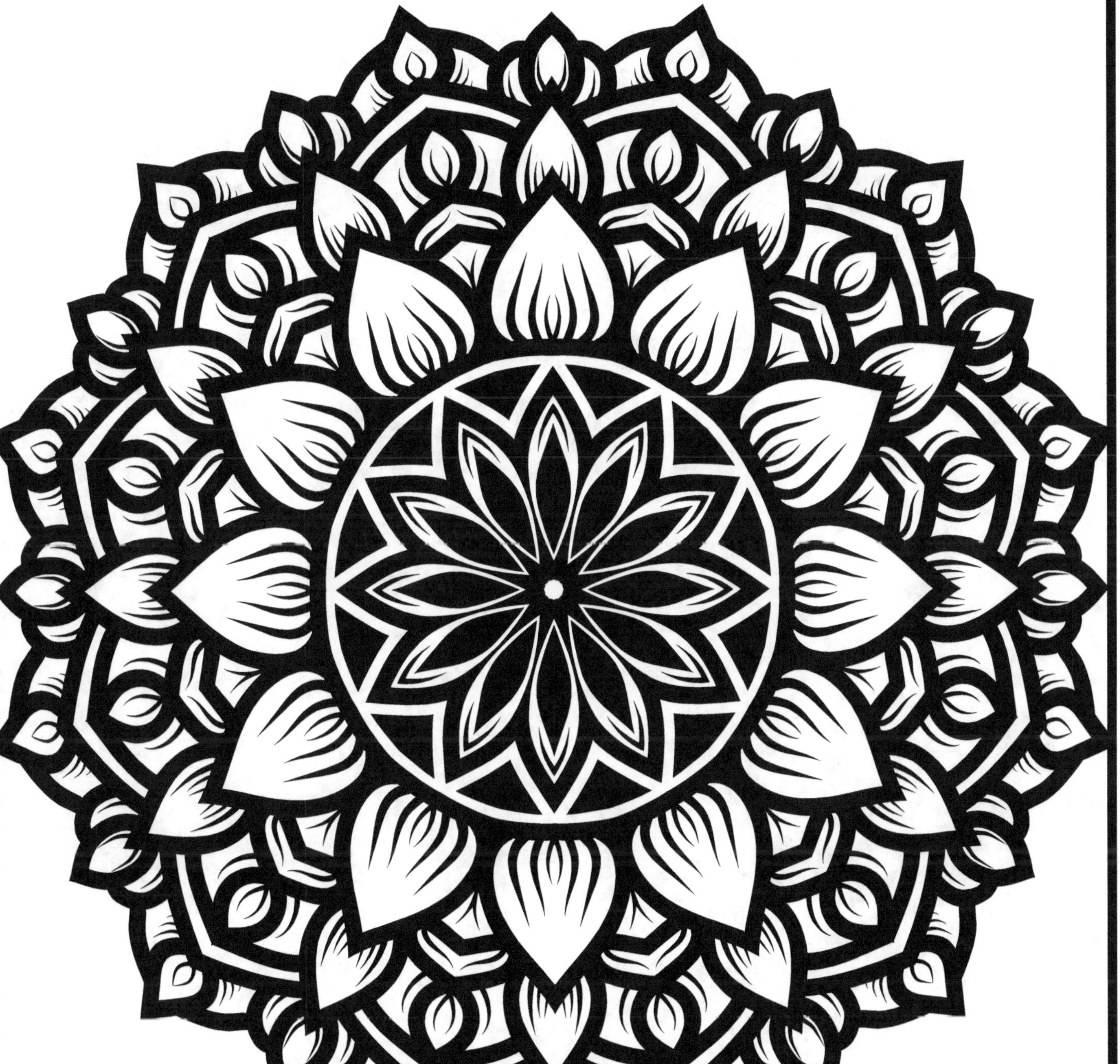
EMBRACE THE CHALLENGE

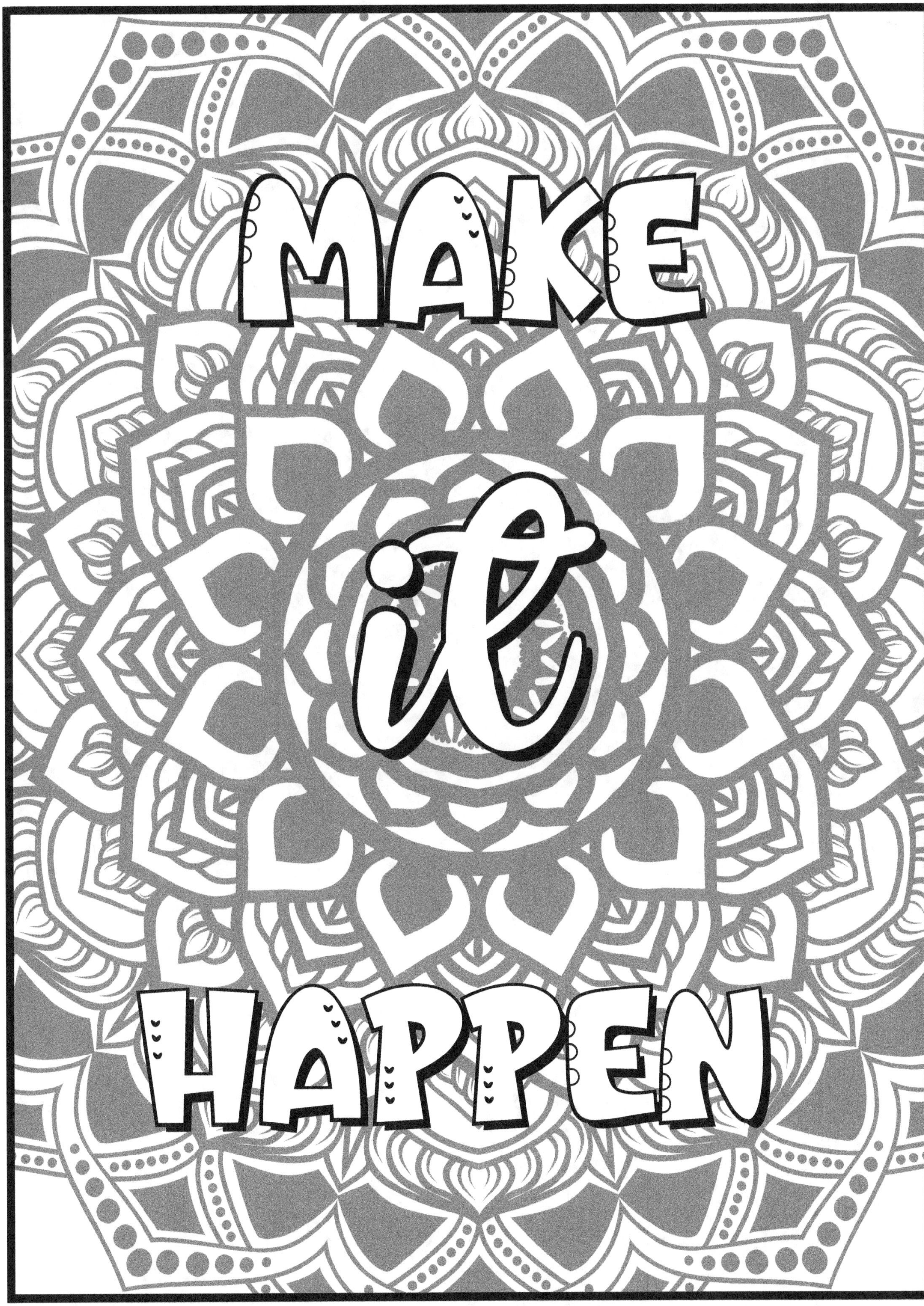
MAKE
it
HAPPEN

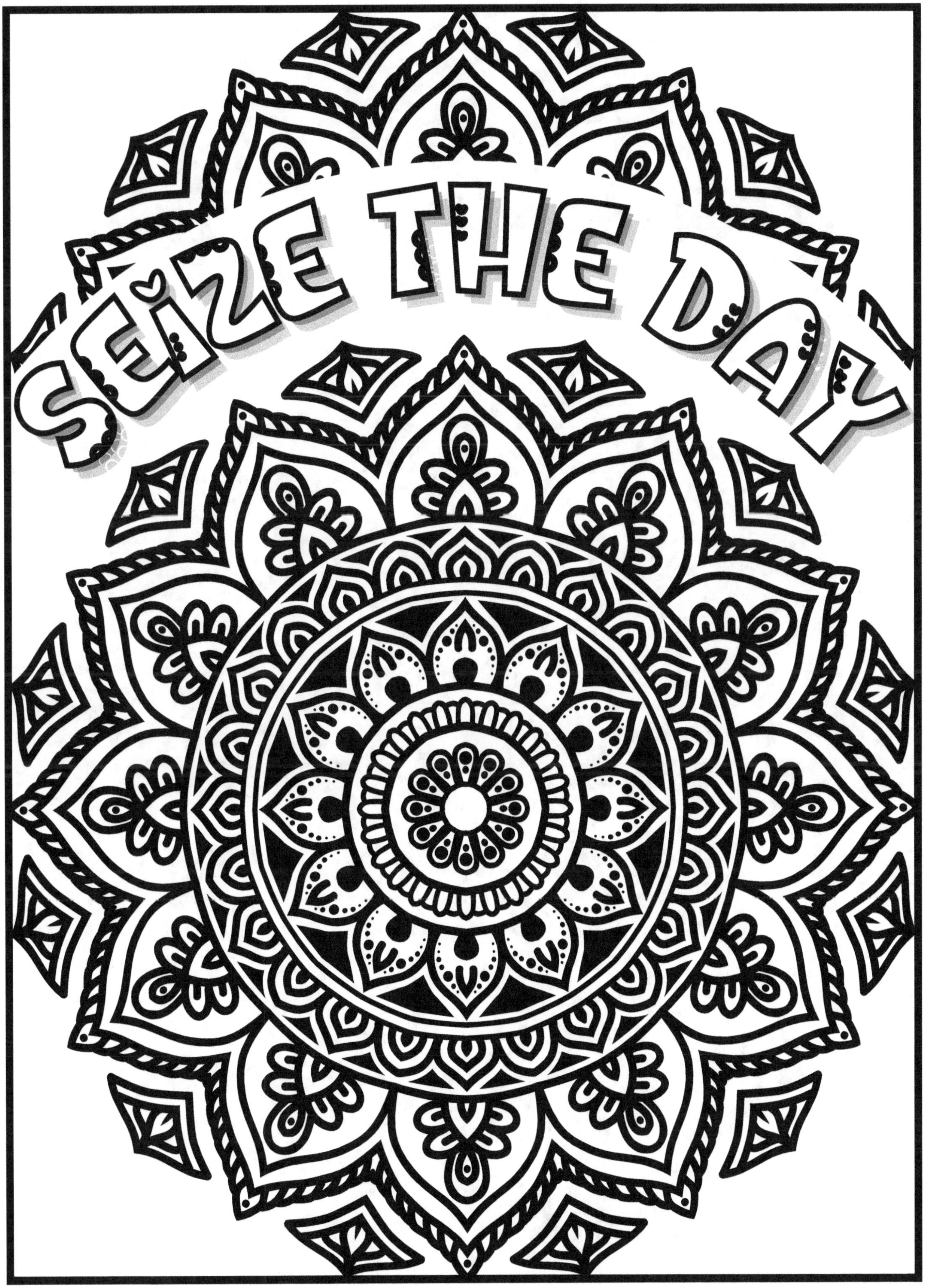
SEIZE THE DAY

STAY HUNGRY

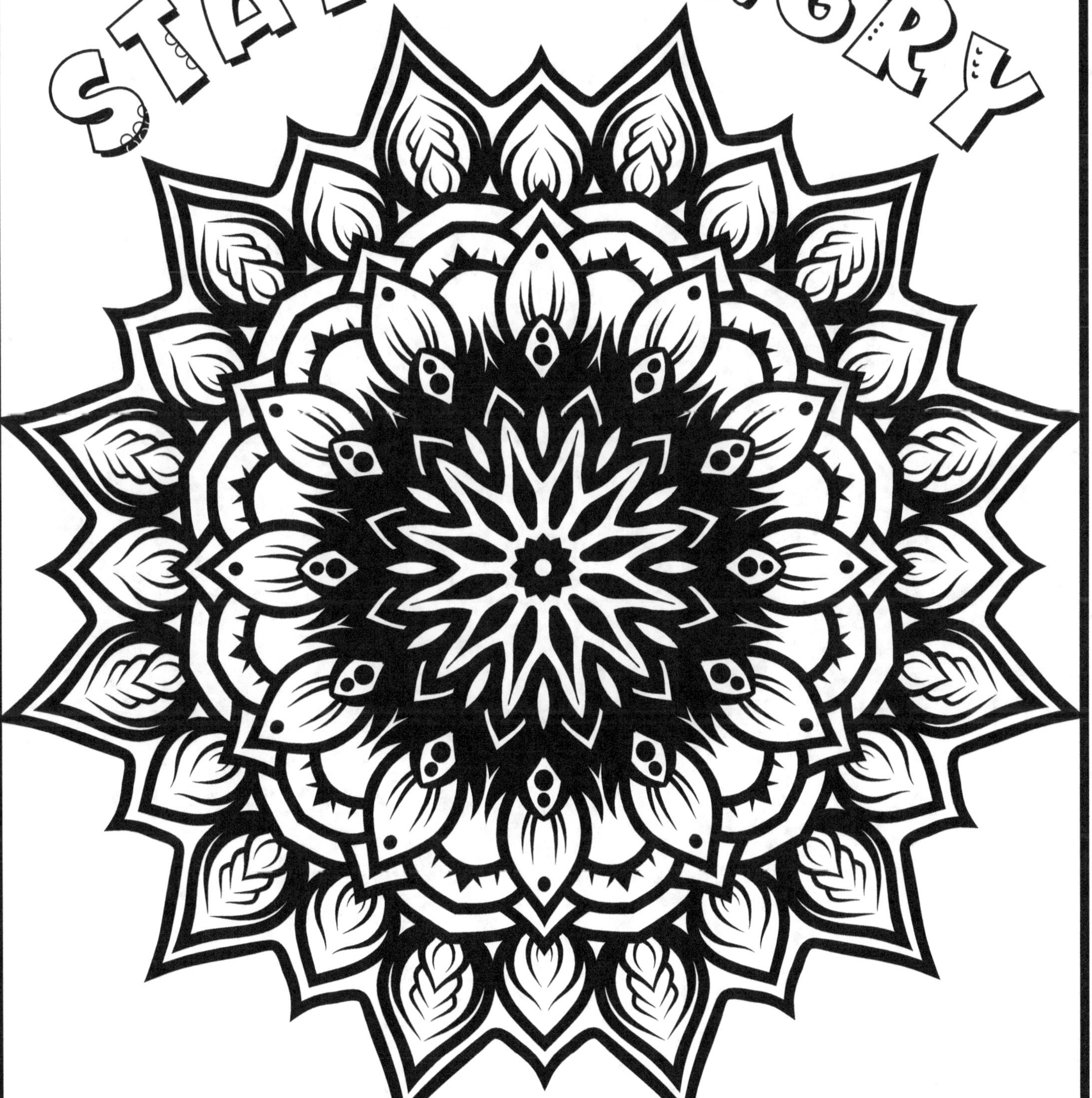

STAY FOOLISH

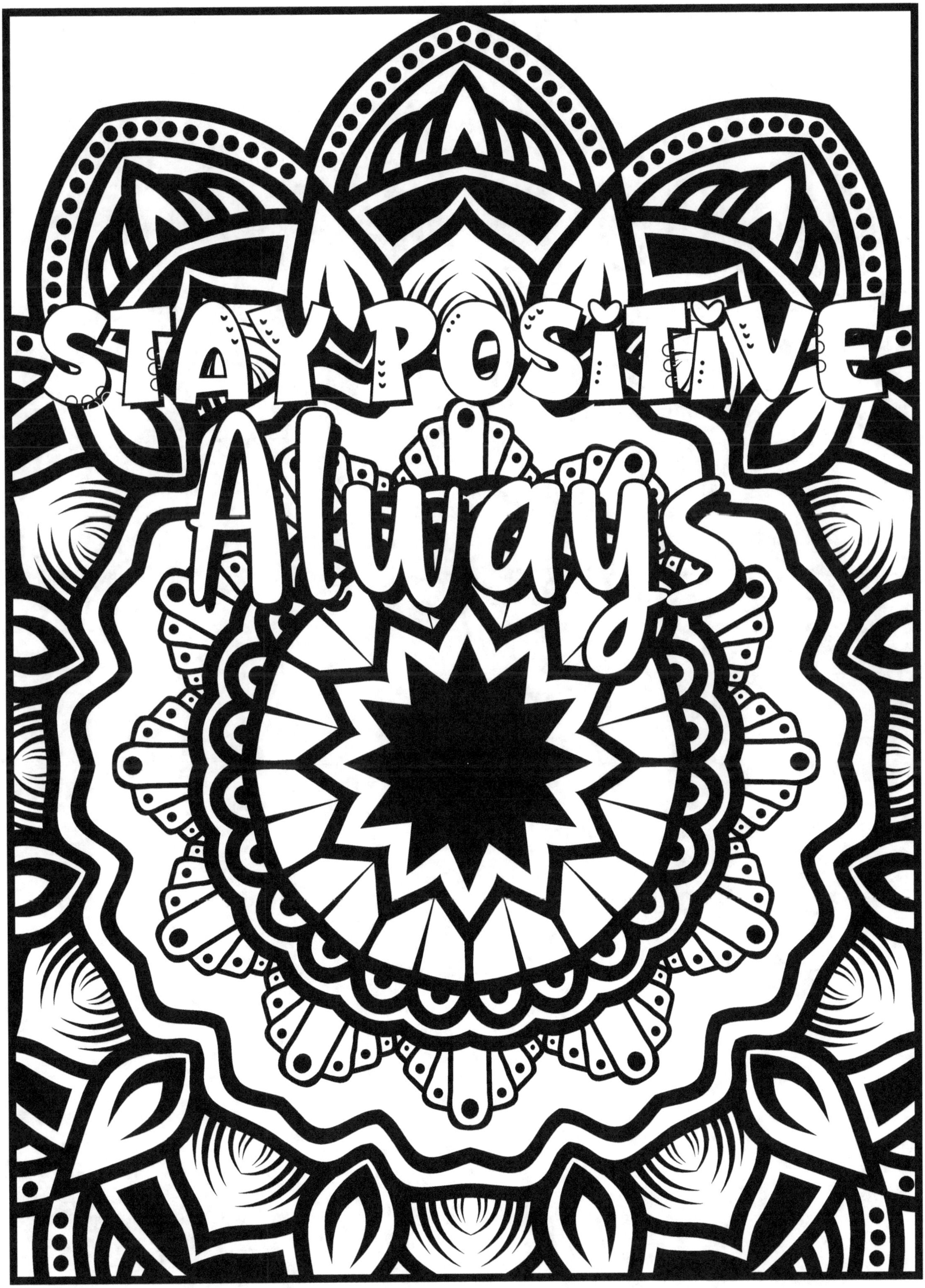
STAY POSITIVE
Always

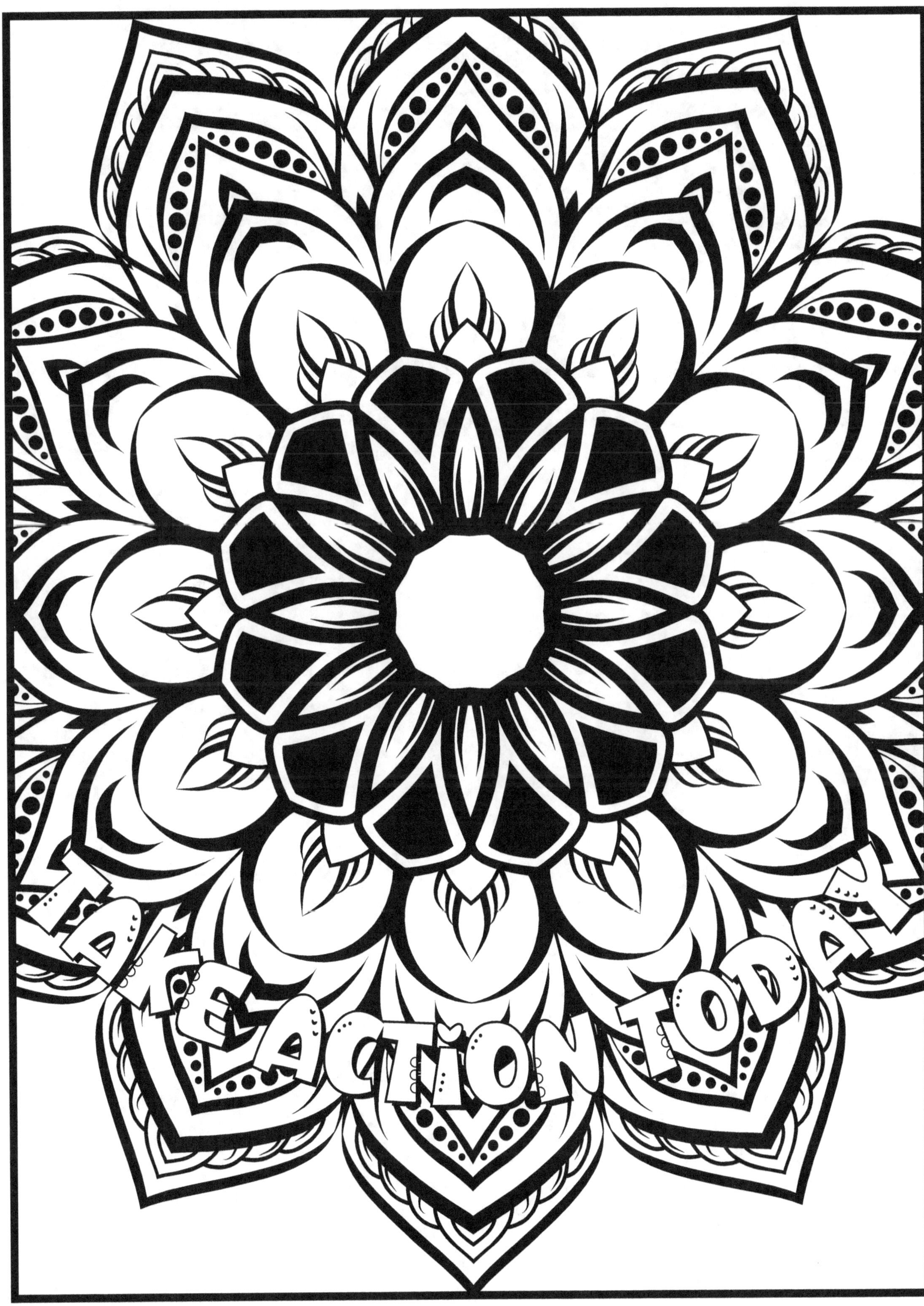
TAKE ACTION TODAY

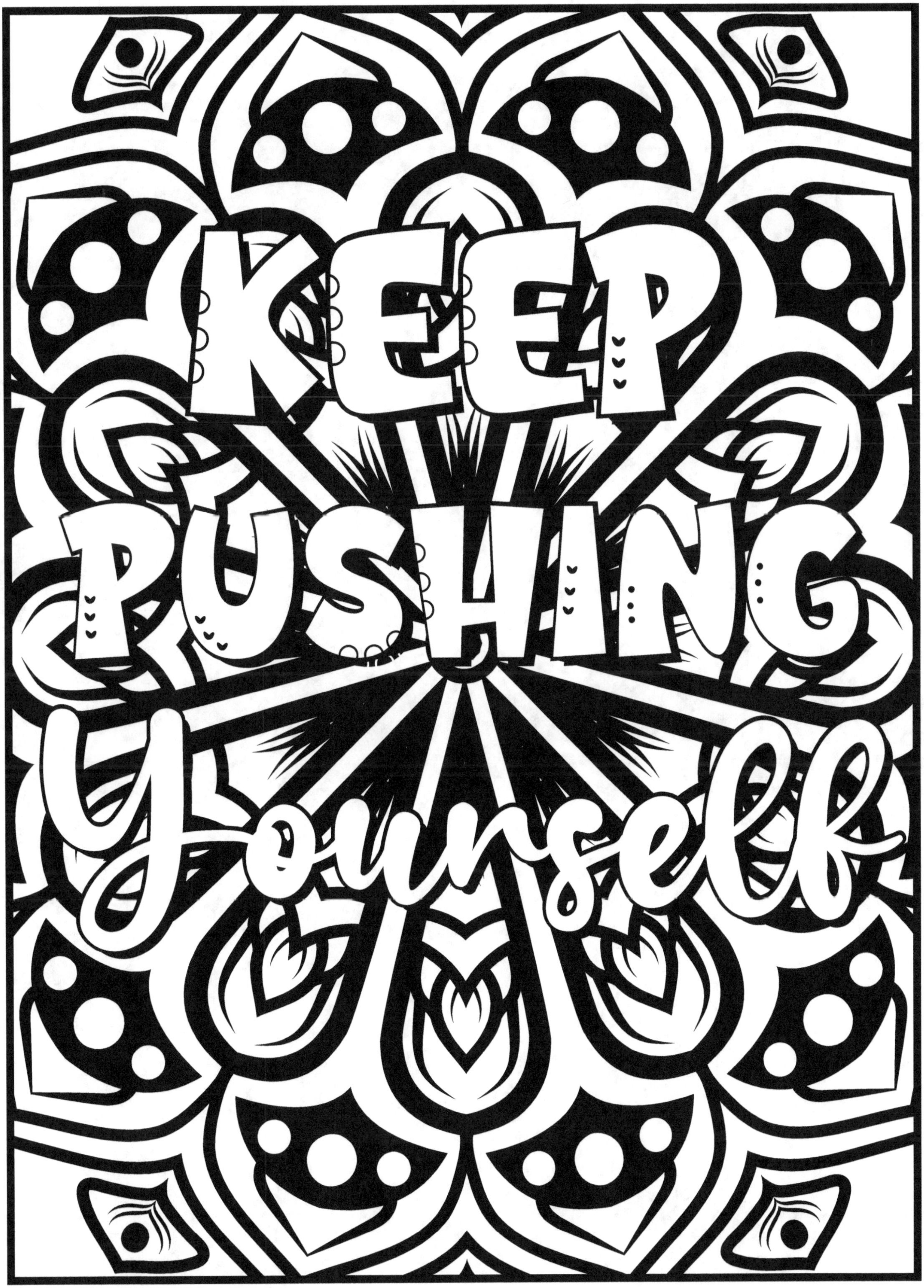
KEEP PUSHING
Yourself

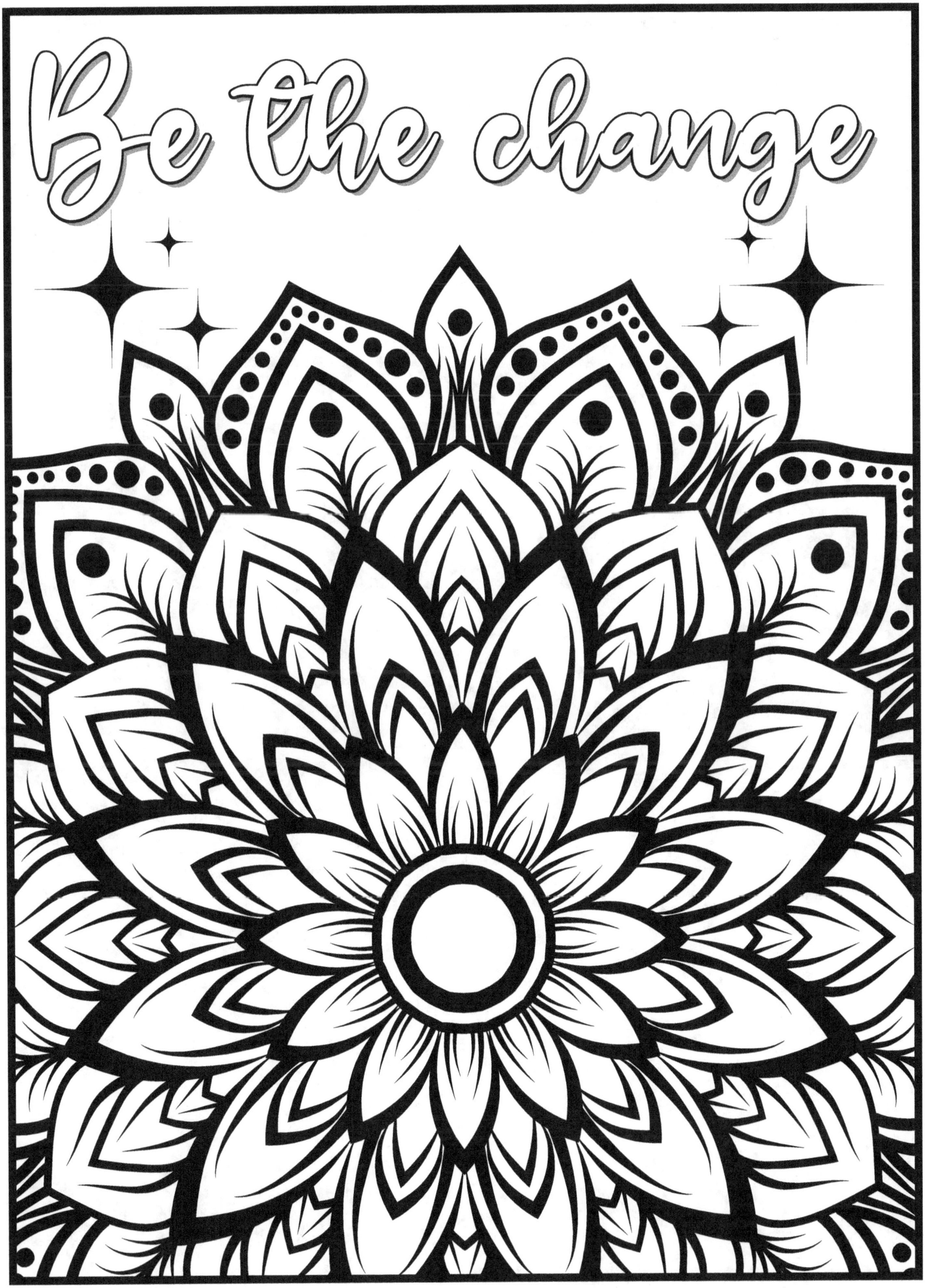
Be the change

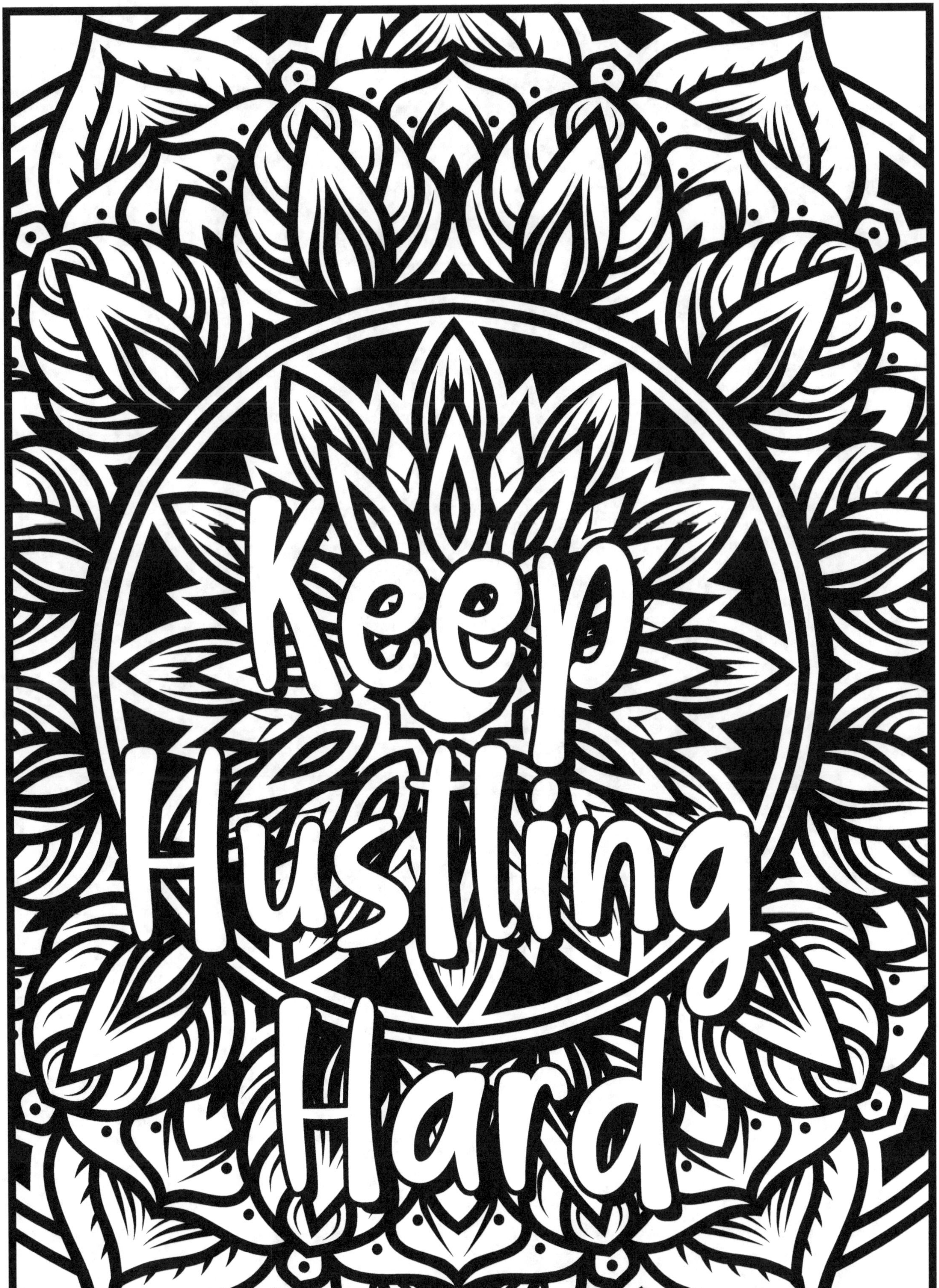
Keep
Hustling
Hard

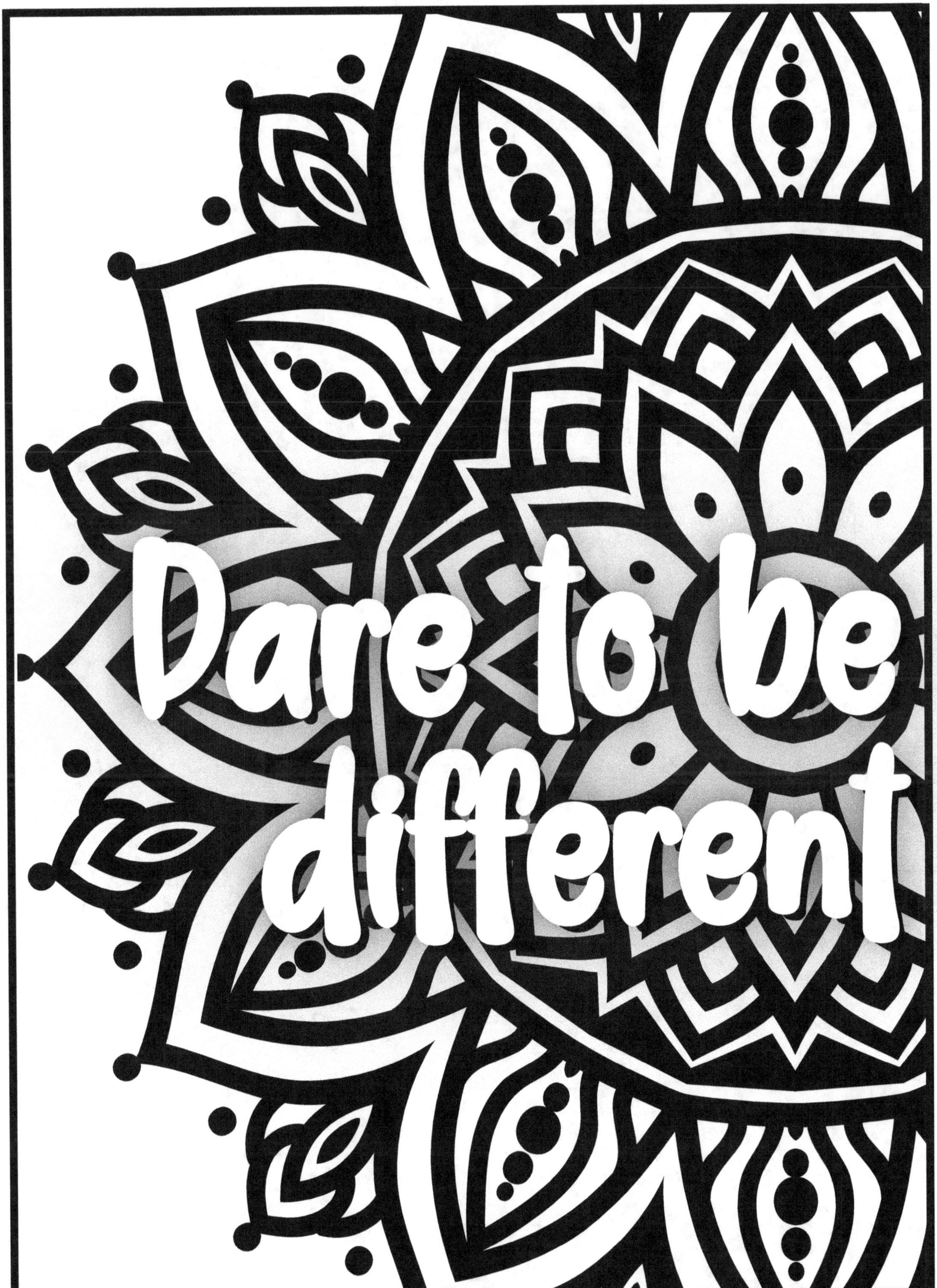
Dare to be
different

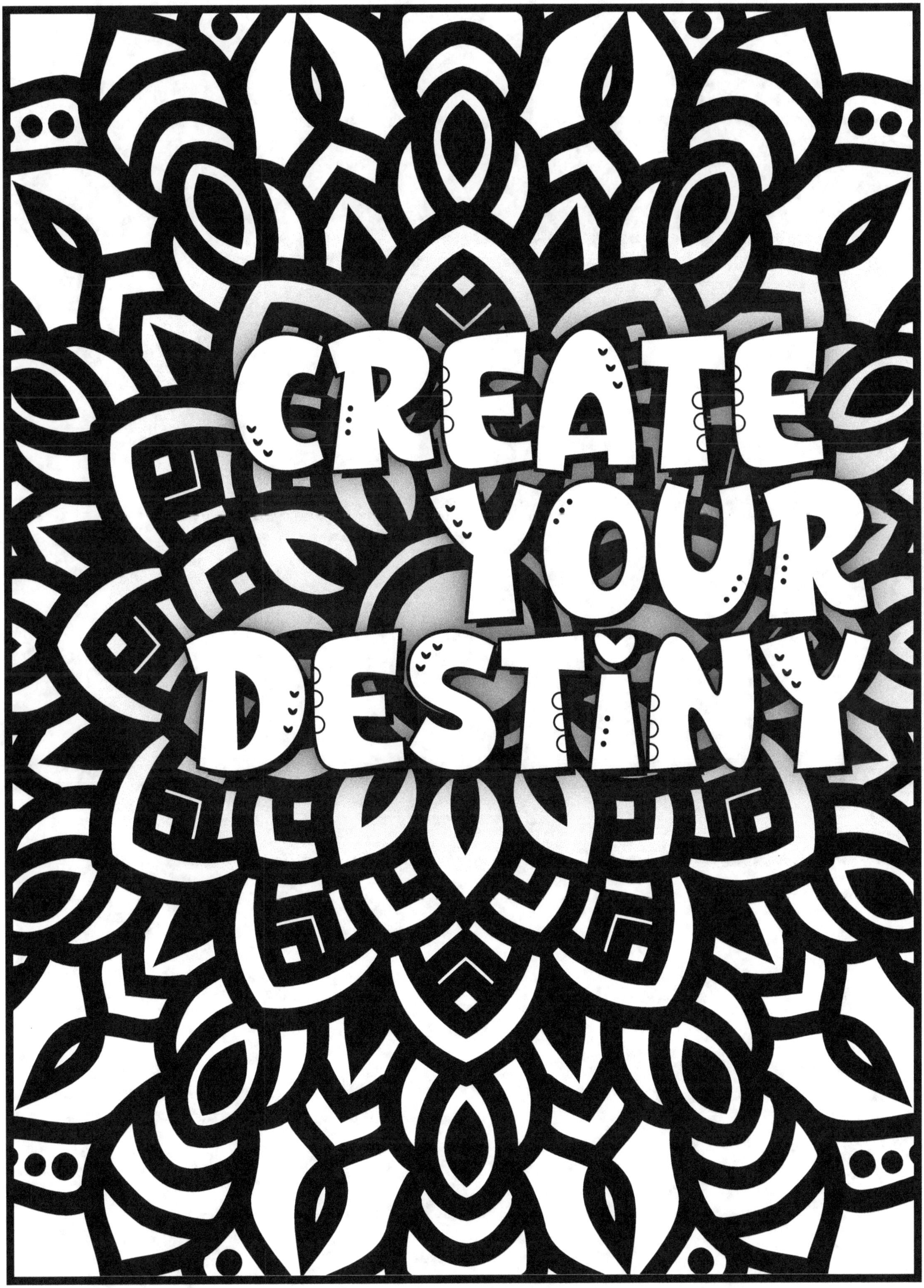
CREATE
YOUR
DESTINY

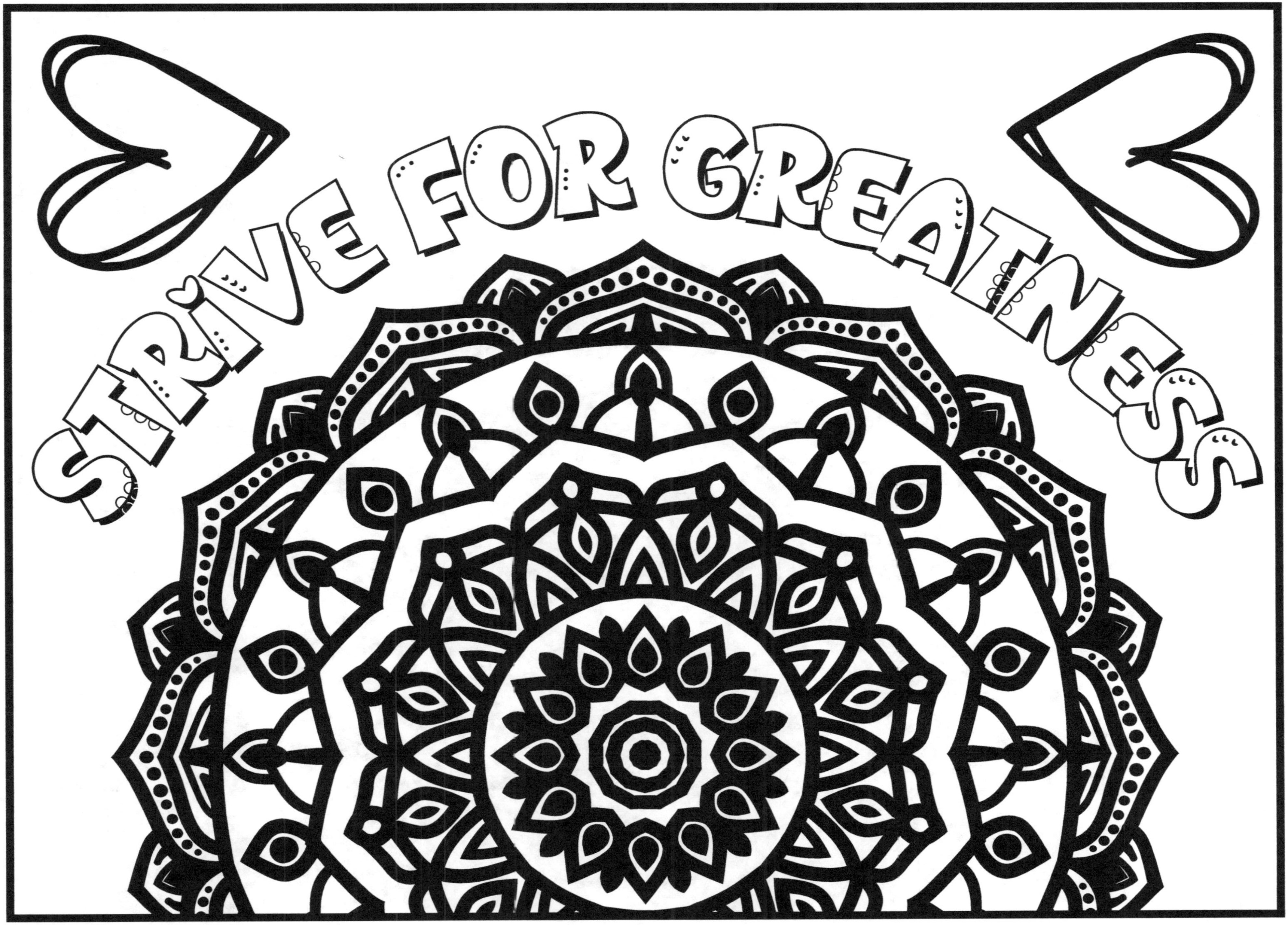
STRIVE FOR GREATNESS

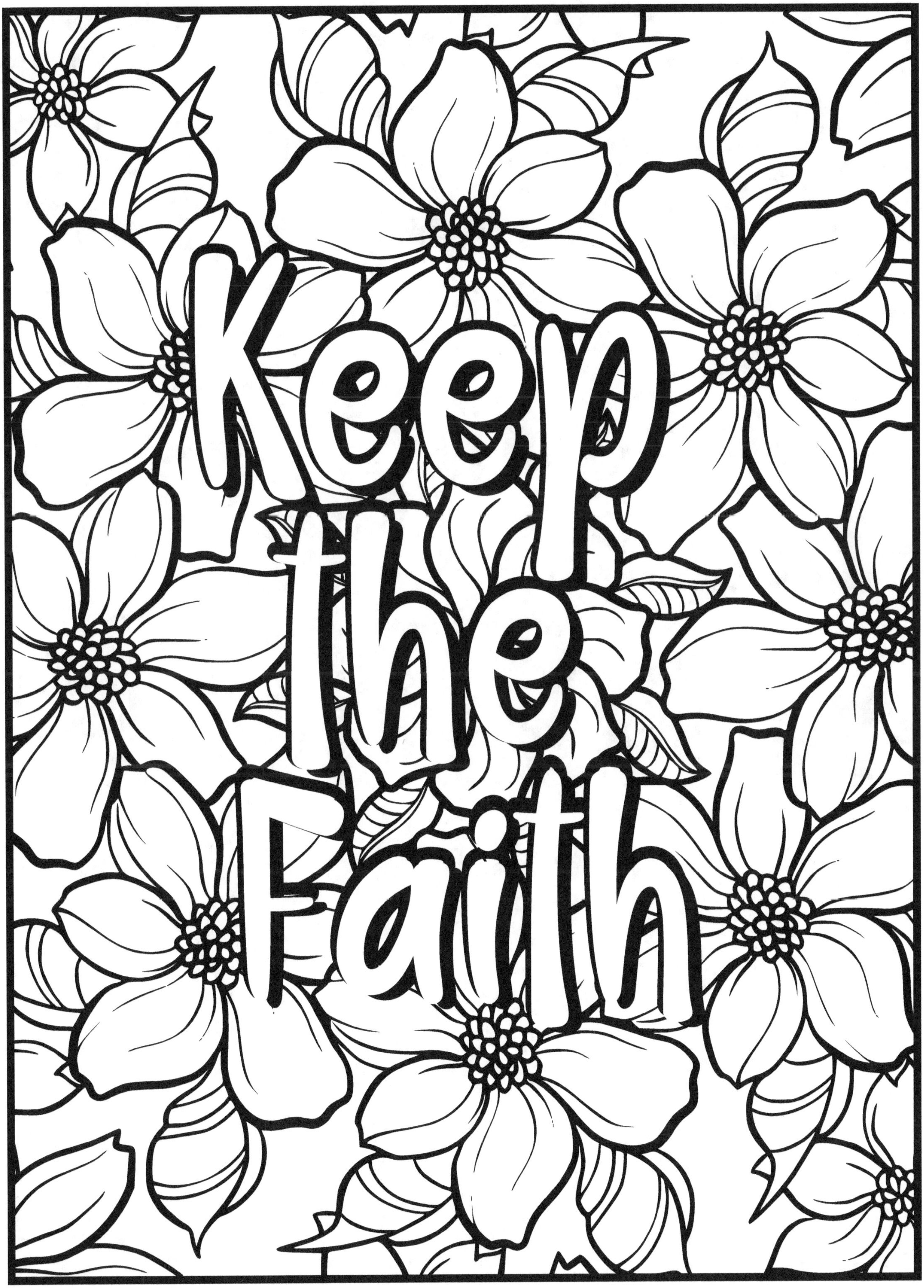
Keep the Faith

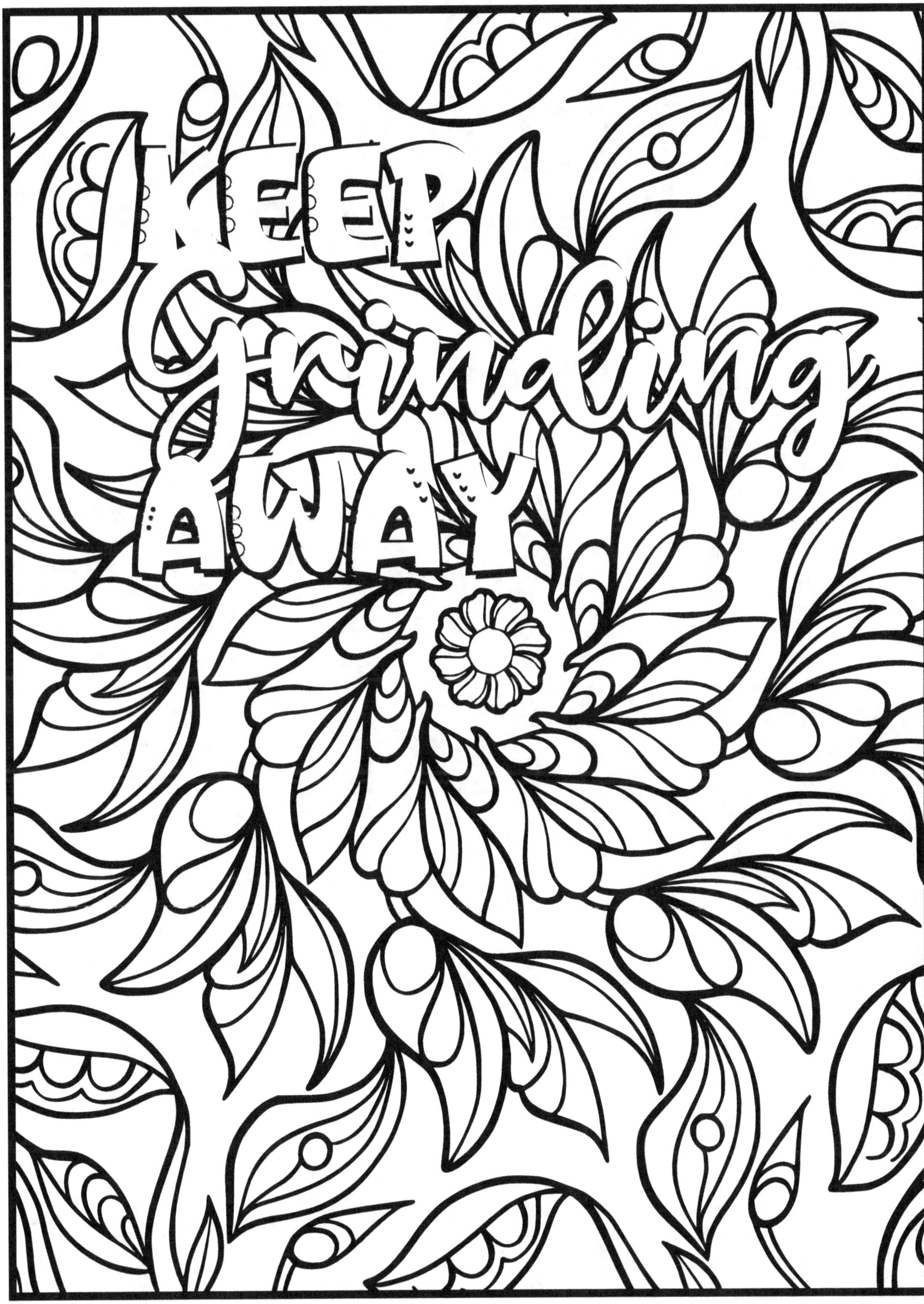
Keep
Grinding
AWAY

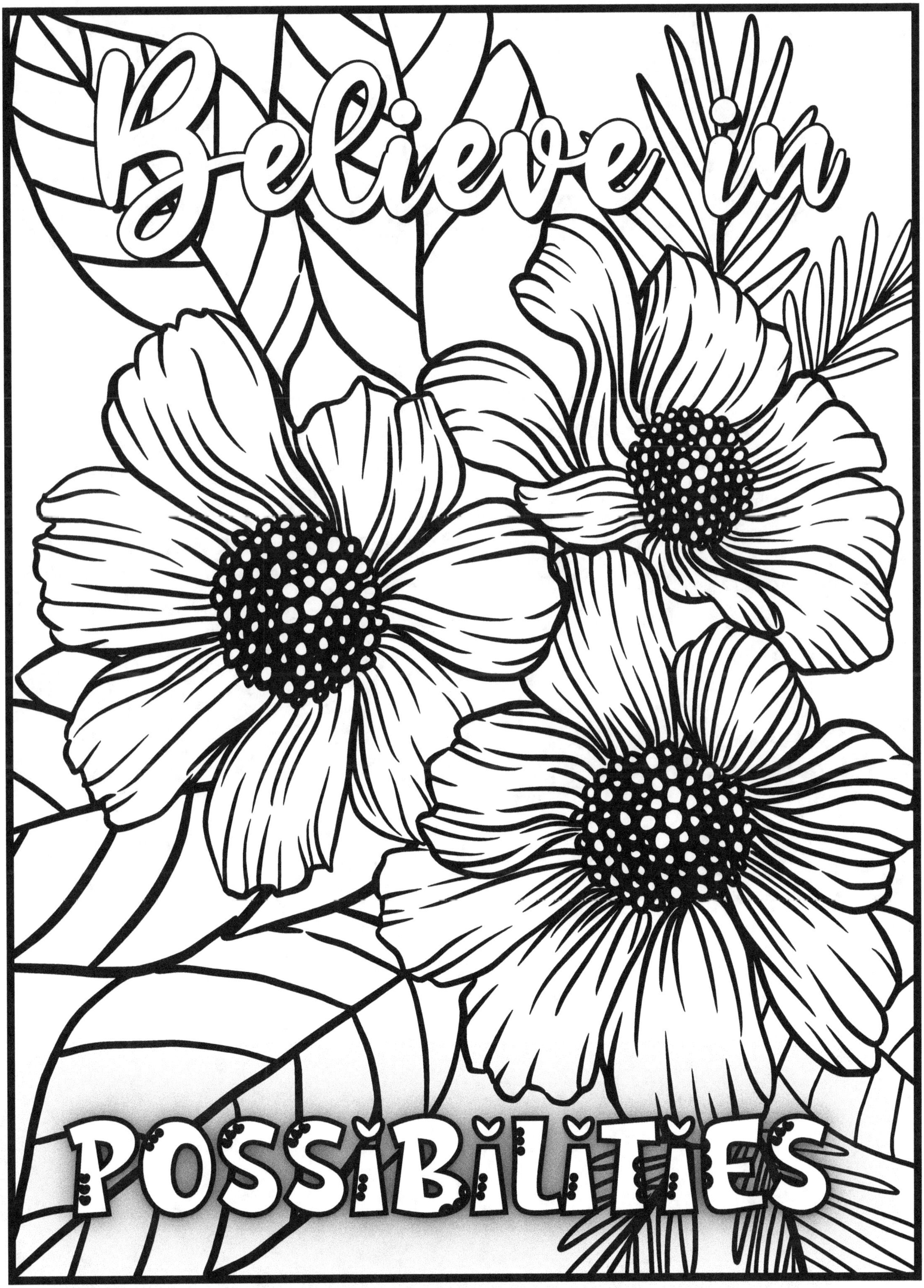
Believe in
POSSIBILITIES

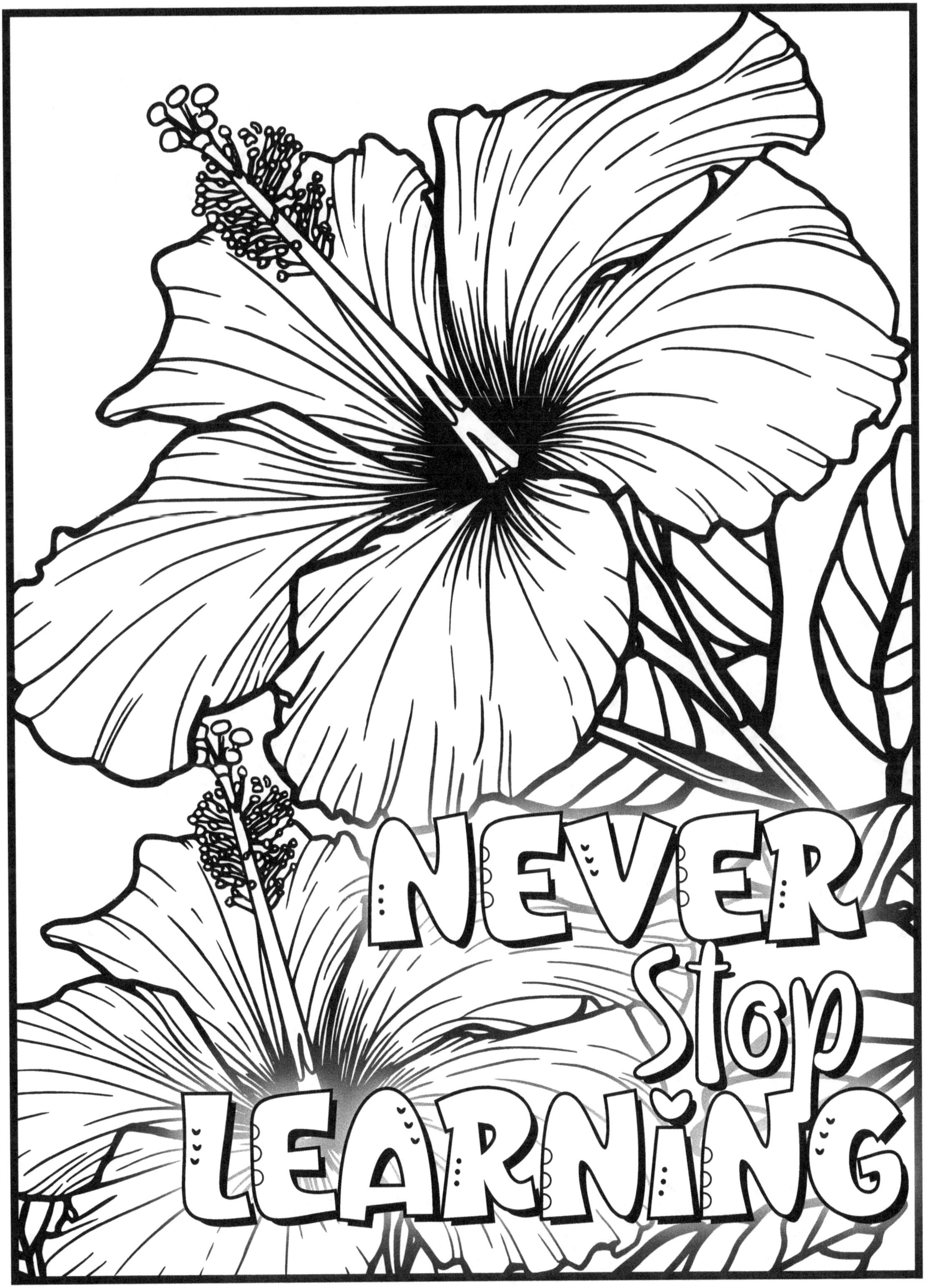
NEVER
Stop
LEARNING

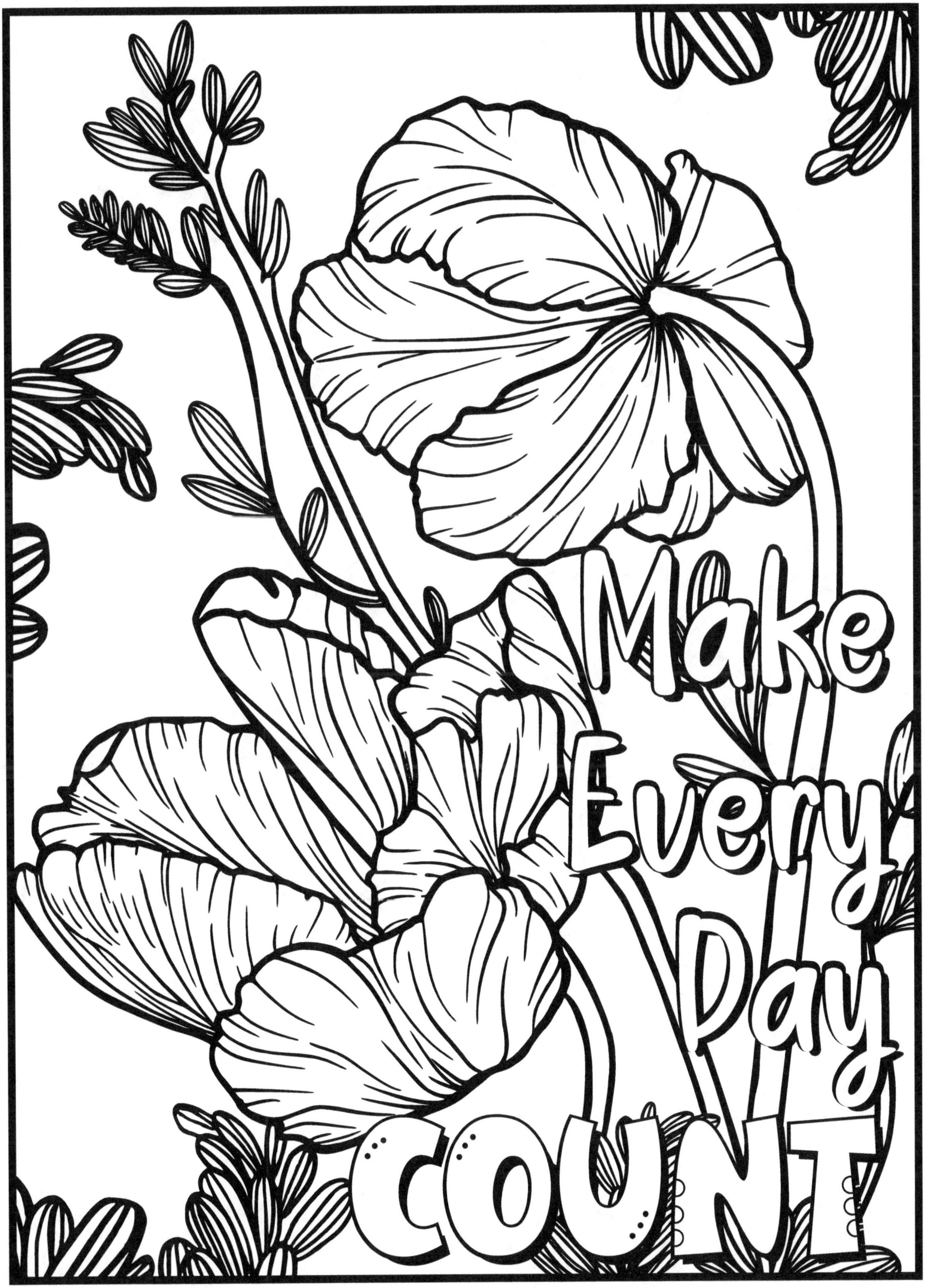
Make
Every
Day
COUNT

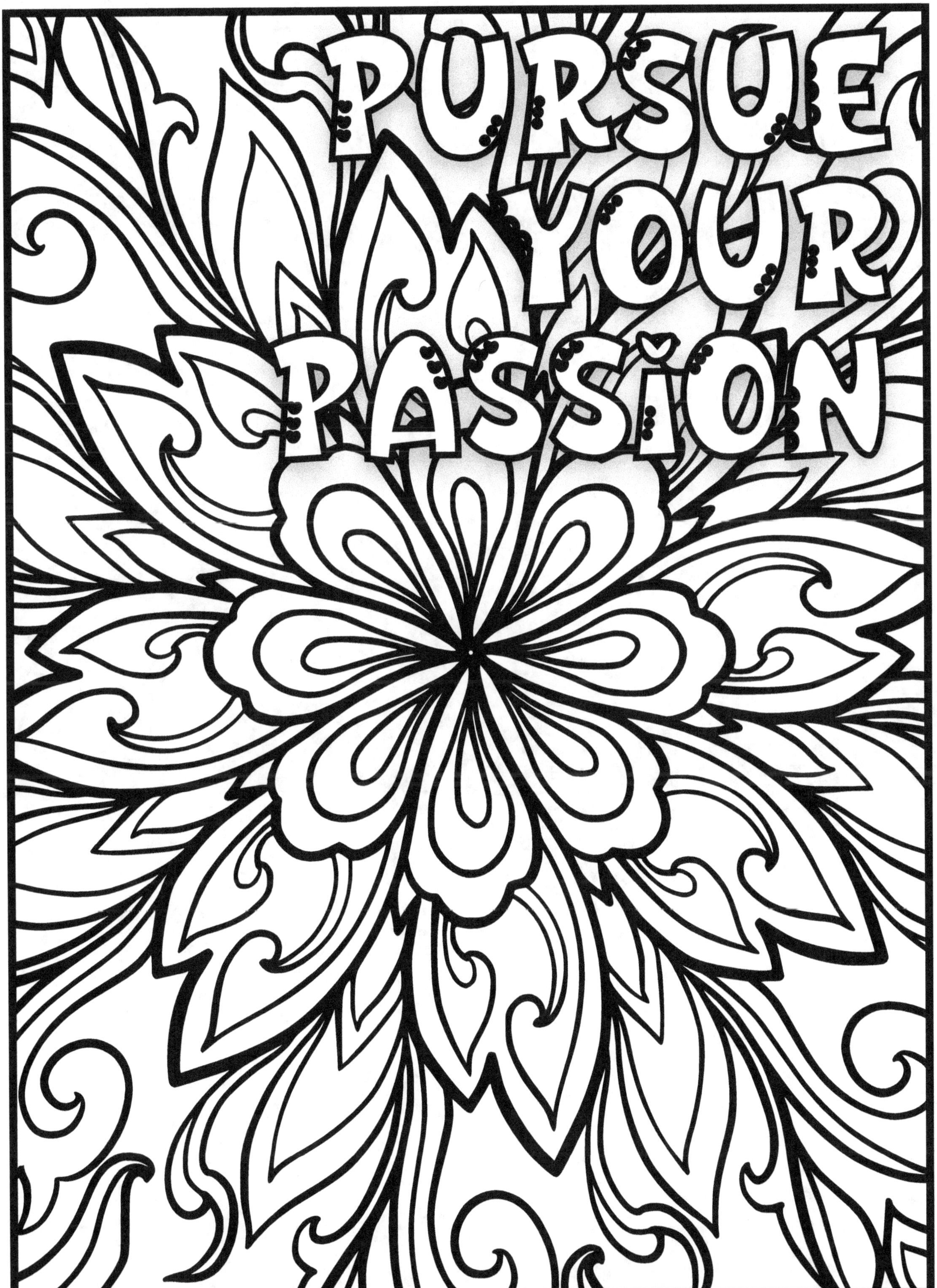
PURSUE
YOUR
PASSION

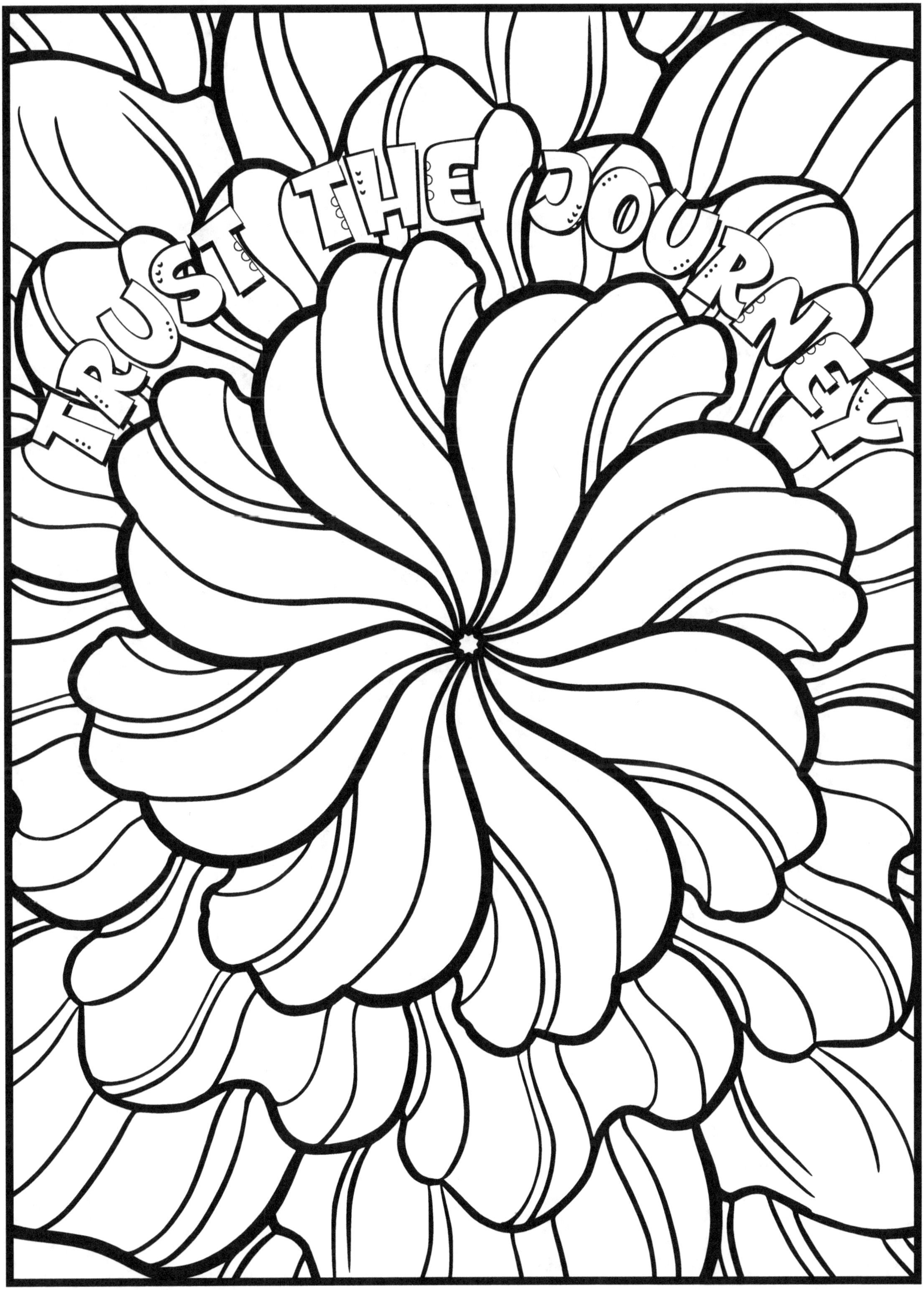
TRUST THE JOURNEY

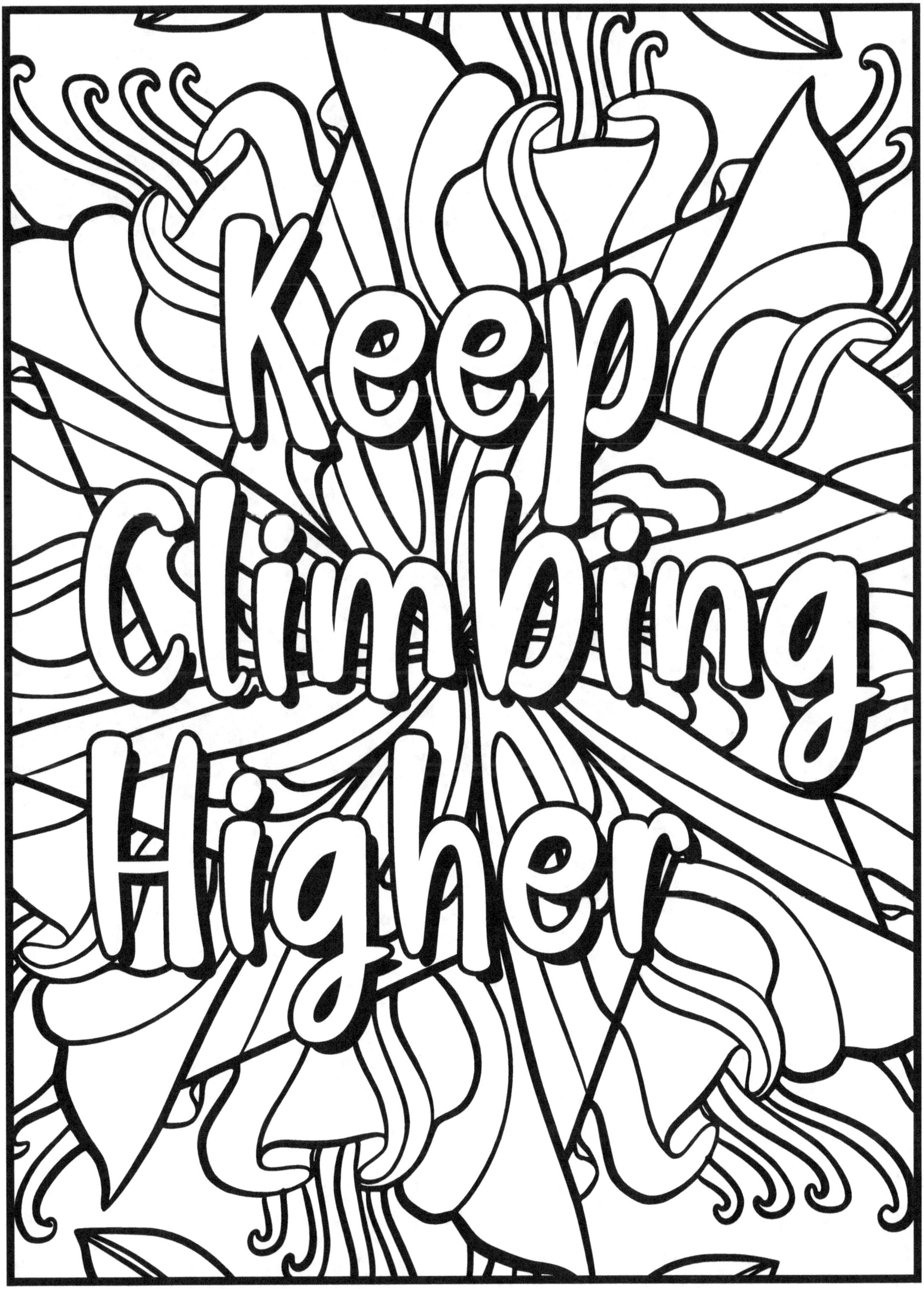
Keep
Climbing
Higher

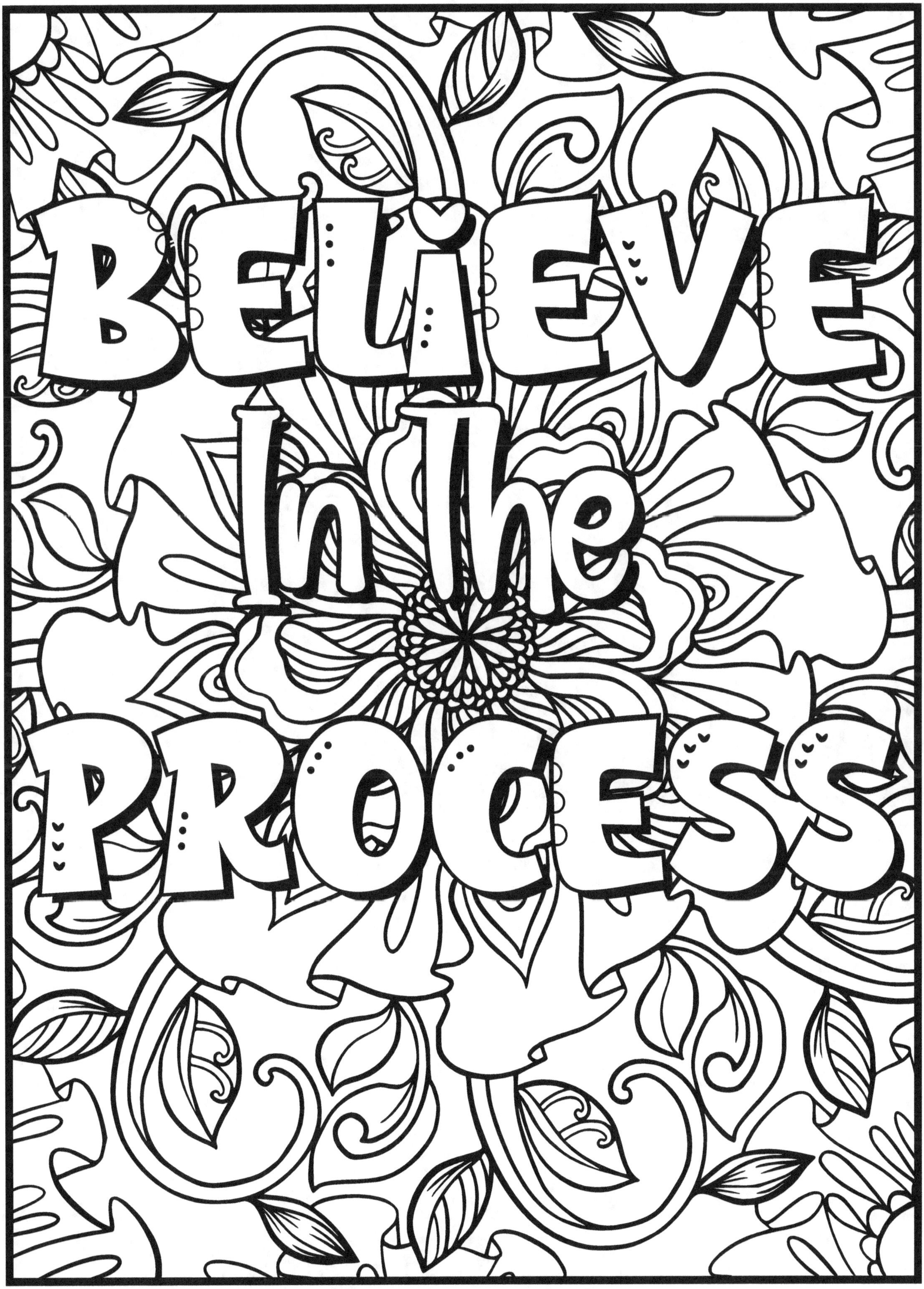
BELIEVE
IN THE
PROCESS

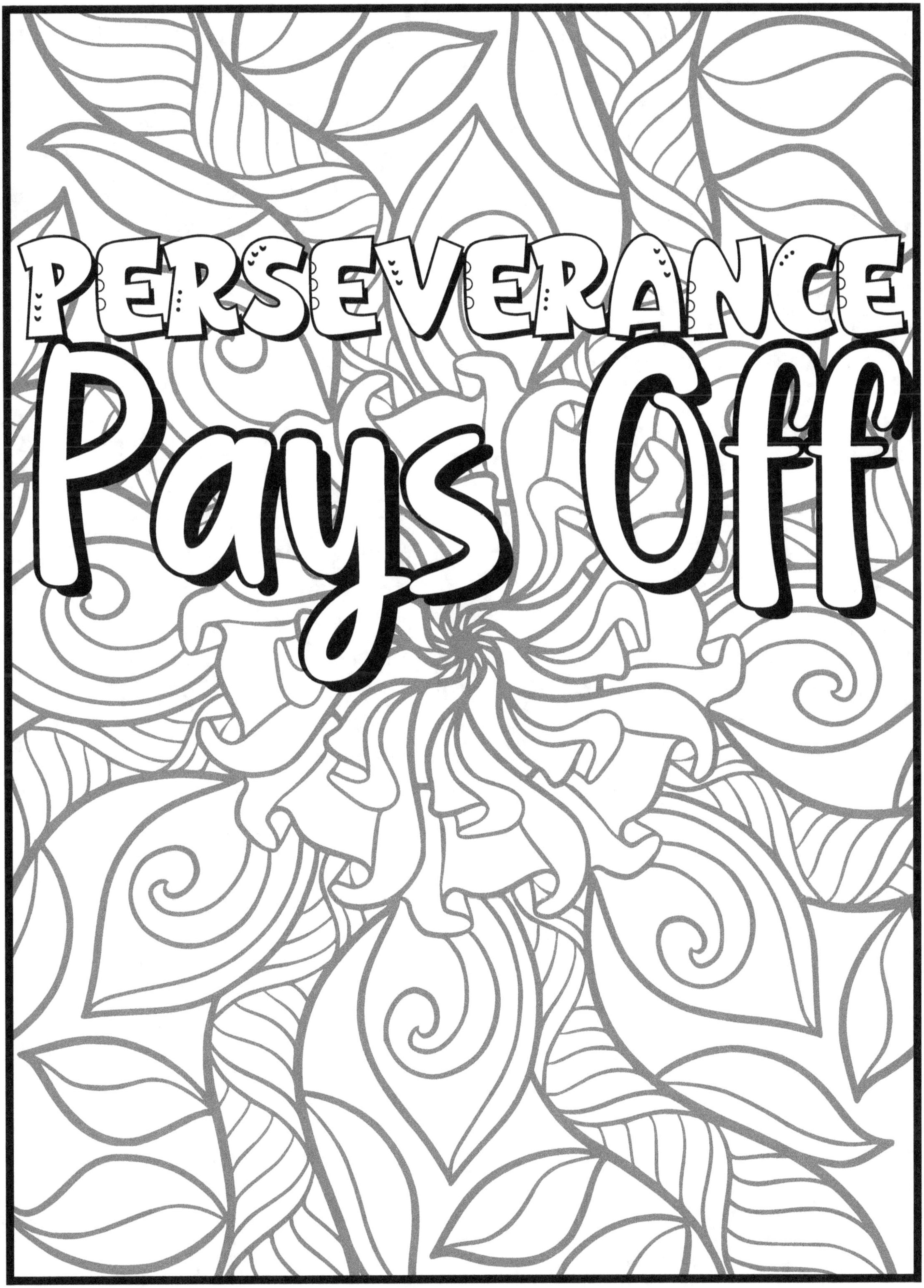
PERSEVERANCE
Pays Off

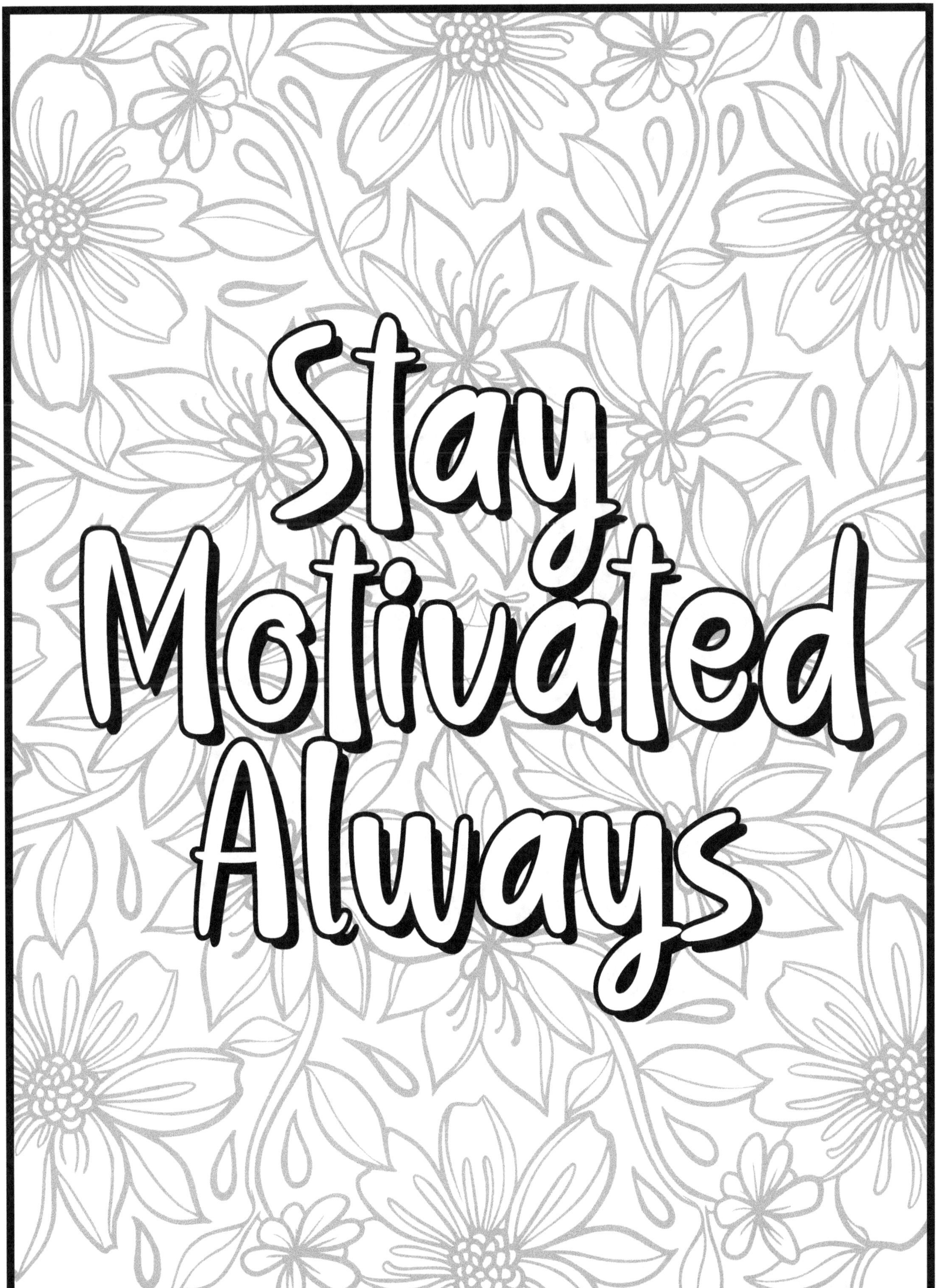
Stay
Motivated
Always

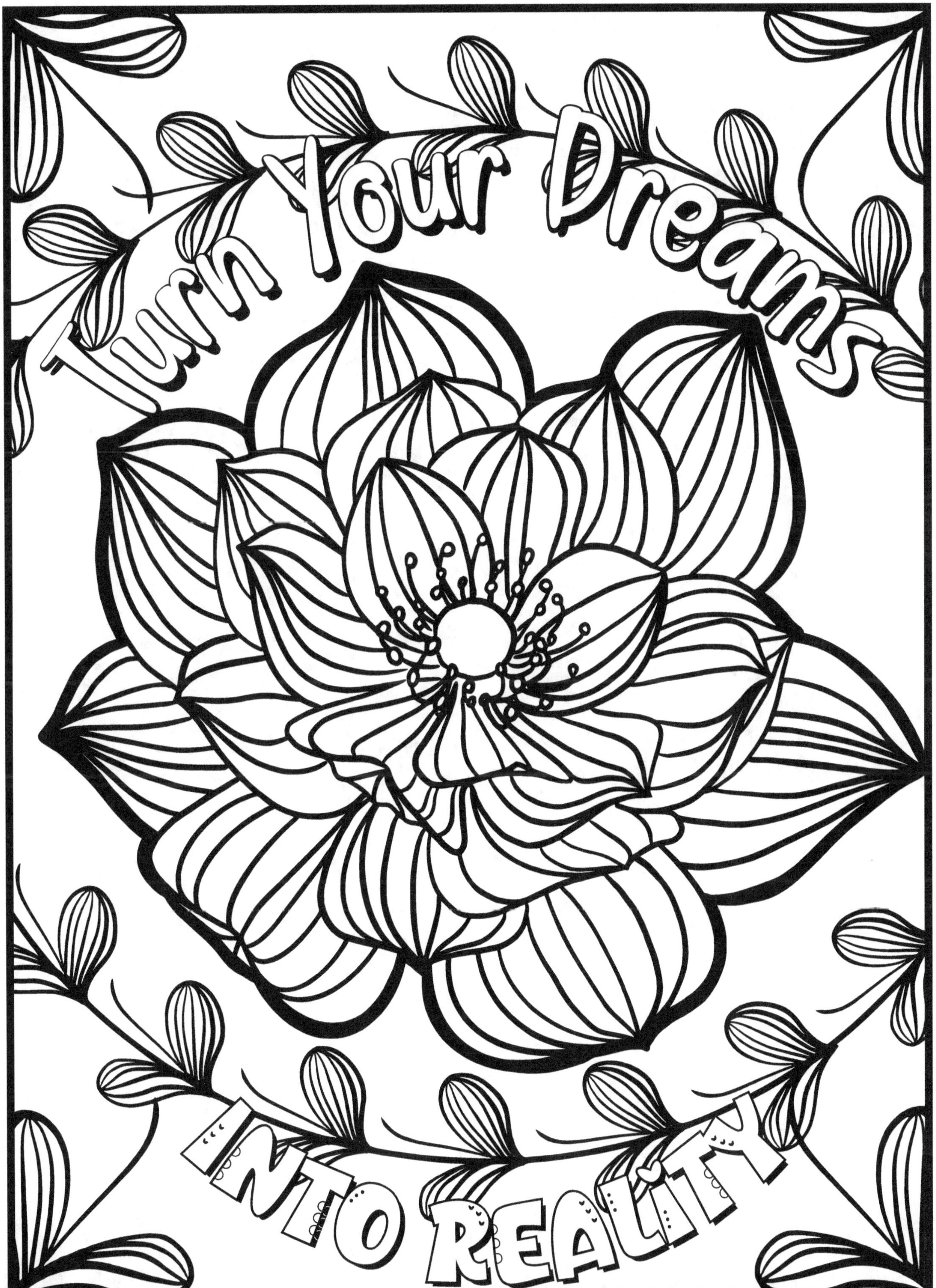
Turn Your Dreams
INTO REALITY

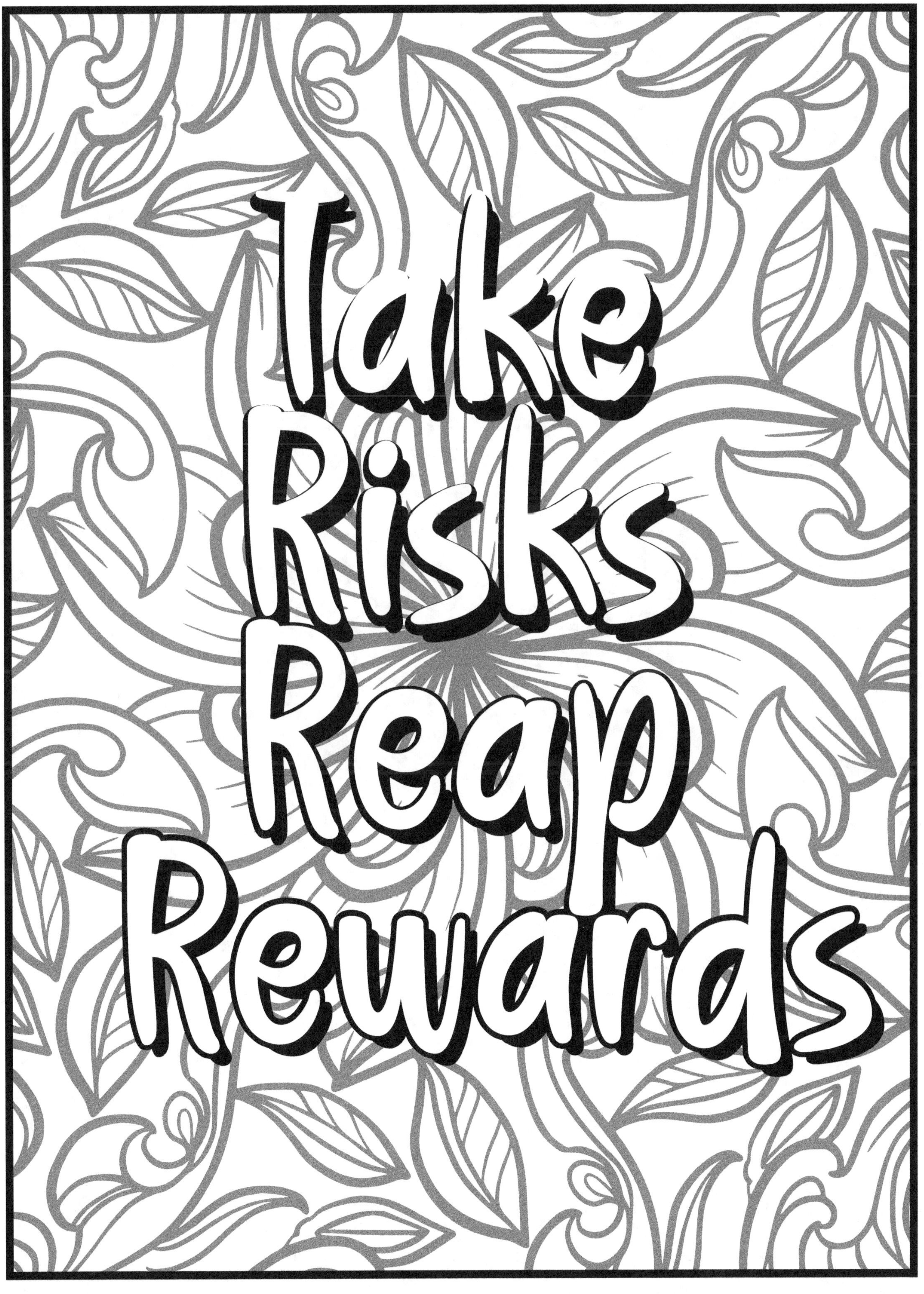
Take
Risks
Reap
Rewards

www.ingramcontent.com/pod-product-compliance
Lightning Source LLC
Chambersburg PA
CBHW080914220526
45467CB00024BA/2652
9798385552054